WEST NILE
Diary

Linda,

I pray you strength for each day,
+ bright hope for tomorrow.

Kathleen G.

One Couple's Triumph
Over a Deadly Disease

WEST NILE
Diary

Kathleen Gibson

Published by
BPS Books
Toronto, Canada
www.bpsbooks.net
A division of Bastian Publishing Services Ltd.

ISBN 978-1-926645-01-8

Cataloguing in Publication Data available from Library and Archives Canada.

Acknowledgments of song lyrics quoted in the text: "Day by Day," Caroline V. Sandell-Berg, 1865, translated by Andrew L. Skoog, 1931. "Hey, Good Lookin'," © 1951 renewed 1979 SONY/ATV-ROSE MUSIC and HIRAM MUSIC. "For the Fruit of All Creation," Fred Pratt Green 1970 © 1970 Hope Publishing Company. "Emmanuel," words and music by Bob McGee, 1976 © 1976 C.A. Music.

Cover and text design: Tannice Goddard, Soul Oasis Networking

Printed by Lightning Source, Tennessee. Lightning Source paper, as used in this book, does not come from endangered old growth forests or forests of exceptional conservation value. It is acid free, lignin free, and meets all ANSI standards for archival-quality paper. The print-on-demand process used to produce this book protects the environment by printing only the number of copies that are purchased.

For Rick, my greatest human treasure,
to help you remember,
and for pirate-fighters everywhere

Preface

Put a clergyman and a writer together in the same crisis and out comes the inevitable: a story with a twist of faith.

It started simply enough.

In August 2007, a mosquito bit my husband.

Early in our journey, I began referring to the virus the bug passed on as "the pirates." This seemed appropriate. As do the henchmen of the sea, the virus attacked his body — and our joint life — violently and without warning, robbing both Rick and me of so much of life's sweet treasure.

We quickly learned something, though. As we battled West Nile neurological disease (WNND), one of North America's newest and most perplexing illnesses, we were never alone. God, as is his habit, came alongside the little boat of our lives. He transformed our journey of desperate physical frailty and emotional upheaval into a deeply spiritual pilgrimage, imprinted at every point with whispers of his miraculous presence.

These pages contain only some of the words that emerged from my pen in the first months following the mosquito bite. I wrote without the benefit of hindsight — though, I see now, not without some measure of divine insight.

Those words, however, needed editing for clarity and for presentation in this format. To do so, I, and my unfailingly patient editor, Donald G. Bastian, waded through a patchwork of material, selecting from journal entries, e-mail updates sent to friends and family, and "Sunny Side Up," my weekly newspaper column published online and in *Yorkton This Week*.

As you read, please note that unless otherwise specified, all dated entries are excerpted from my journal.

⌒

This is our story, and this how it unfolded. But it's not our story alone. We encountered others along the way: fellow patients, their families and friends, staff. Some had also been attacked, often in a split second, by their own pirates (or monsters, madmen, or beasts). You'll meet a few of them between these covers, too. (I wish we could have included them all — perhaps next time!)

I've learned three things in my journey down the West Nile with Rick and the pirates: God is a lot stronger than I thought he was, I'm a lot stronger than I thought I was, and God can do exquisite things with broken circumstances. If you're fighting pirates of whatever stripe, read fast and read deep. In a sense, this is the gospel according to the pirates, and God may use it for your soul's healing.

⌒

Allow me to express Rick's and my profound gratitude to God and those he has used — is still using — to help us in our fight against West Nile neurological disease. We are grateful for ...

The unexpected graces of complete strangers and new friends (including Rick's fellow patients and their families), who followed the pirates up the gangplank and deposited more treasure than the scoundrels stole.

The kindness, patience, encouragement, and friendship of the medical personnel we met on our journey.

The prayers, love, and generous support of family, friends, community, and church on four continents.

Those who have kindly allowed me to include them and their stories between these covers.

May God bless each of you in the same measure that you have blessed us.

Kathleen and Rick Gibson

P.S. Wear repellent!

Introduction

On a burnished golden day in the fall of 2007, I fled to the shore of a small lake in Regina, Saskatchewan, two hours southwest of our home in Yorkton. Overhead, flocks of Canada geese were assembling into their vees, pointing them south, and honking their farewells.

Plopping down on a wood-slatted bench, I noticed another flock of geese grazing nearby, fattening up for their southward migration. As I watched, a large goose ambled near my bench. The bird seemed unperturbed by its plight: Its left wing was sticking almost straight up.

Two able-bodied companions flanked their wounded comrade solicitously as it pecked its way across the grass.

The disabled creature was the third broken-left-winged bird to enter my life over the previous twelve months.

I had noticed the second one in the summer from the window of our rented lakeside cottage, about half an hour from home. My fifty-four-year-old husband, Rick, known as the Preacher in the prairie city where we had served the same Nazarene congregation for sixteen years, lay in the bedroom behind me. He was recovering, or so we hoped, from what two doctors had diagnosed as a bad case of the flu and a severe sinus infection.

That bird (also a Canada goose) had walked along the lakeshore, dragging its drooping wing on the grass, staring at its able-bodied flock-mates bobbing like corks in the distance. It didn't call them, nor did it try to go out to them. Finally, in a rocking motion designed to arrange the awkward wing as comfortably as possible, it settled down on the shore.

Its presence chilled me to the core.

I had found the first of this wounded threesome of birds while walking our back lane the winter previous to Rick's eventual diagnosis of West Nile disease. Its wing was so badly mangled, I knew it would never fly again. I brought it home to die.

But the Bohemian waxwing had other ideas. With the hardy pluck so often found in the least among us, it lived. Its broken wing bone finally fell off entirely, but the bird began singing about a week after I brought it home. All winter, it cheered me and all who entered our home with its attempts to pass raisins to its buddy in the mirror, its exquisite trills, its indomitable spirit.

For the entire time that we hosted our diminutive feathered guest, I felt I must pay close attention: that I would soon need the lessons I was learning while I cared for it. Lessons of compassion and trust, love and relinquishment.

The waxwing did die while in my care — suddenly, head thrown back, mid-song — but not until six months later. I grieved for that bird with hard, hot tears from a depth I didn't know I contained.

Three birds. Three broken left wings. God had begun teaching both Rick and me the beauty of brokenness.

Wednesday, August 15

Rick woke in the night, padded to the bathroom, and began shaking uncontrollably. Back in bed, he couldn't get warm. During the day he complained of a vicious headache.

Thursday, August 16

Rick's headache won't go away, and he felt nauseous all day. When he wasn't out on church business, he came home to rest. He seems to have a fever. He can't stop sweating. He didn't eat.

Friday, August 17

His flu is no better. He ate nothing worth talking about today, and the headache and nausea still haven't left. He went out but came home exhausted and slept through meals. He hasn't been able to exercise on the treadmill since Wednesday.

When I gave him a cup of tea today, he needed both hands to pick it up. Says his fingertips feel numb, and his left arm is getting weak.

Saturday, August 18

The grandbeans (Benjamin, two and a half, Tabatha, one) visited today while their mama (our daughter, Amanda) shopped. Rick did come to the table at our request, but managed only to sit, with his aching head in his hands.

Benjamin said, "Gampa?" a few times, then, "Gampa seeping?"

He's already learned to worry. I saw it in his eyes.

After they left this evening, Rick sat down at the computer, read a while, and finally said, very slowly, "You know, hon, I seem to have all the symptoms of West Nile."

I read the page he had up on the screen. Excruciating headache. Astonishing joint and muscle pain. High fever. Nausea.

He's still having some difficulty holding things or lifting his cup of tea. His left arm is too weak, he says, and it shakes.

"Let's get it checked out," I said.

We waited for over three hours in an examining room at our local hospital. He lay down, and I sat beside him, thinking how much I needed that sick man on the bed. All the worst-case scenarios galloped through my mind.

"Hon, you should have brought a book," he said softly.

"Why would I want to read when I can sit here and worry?" I asked.

He groaned.

The doctor did finally come in, in a terrible hurry. He didn't glance my way. Said, by way of greeting, "What's the problem?"

Rick gave a thorough list of his symptoms: headache, nausea, joint pain, muscle weakness, fever, trembles.

"I think I may have West Nile," he said.

The doctor checked Rick's eyes, ears, chest, and throat, told him he had the flu and added, "You don't have West Nile. You have a bad sinus infection." He prescribed antibiotics, and sent us home. He had spent about two minutes in the room.

Sunday, August 19

Rick, still feeling terrible, took a sick day today. Tomorrow, God willing, we leave for Tranquil Acres. It's only half an hour from home, but that rented cottage beside tiny Theodore Lake will be a good place to recover.

Monday, August 20
Tranquil Acres

He felt worse today, sweating and aching like crazy. Too weak to get dressed. Before leaving town I took him to see Jan Coetzee, our doctor and family friend. He concurred with the emergency doctor and said the antibiotics prescribed should help. He ordered blood tests.

"Come back on Wednesday if he's not feeling better," he said.

Back home, Rick watched, miserable, as I prepared for our trip.

"I'm sorry, hon," he said, as he watched me lugging out bags and suitcases and boxes of food to the car. "I feel so bad I can't help you."

"Hey, it's my turn," I said. "How many years have you done this all by yourself?"

And off we went, though with markedly less anticipation than usual.

Concerned members of our congregation called throughout the day to find out how he is. Lovely, but tiring. With no phone here, he can have absolute rest.

The weather delivered clouds and rain for our trip. But by the time we arrived, the clouds had thinned, making room for a glorious sunset. I unpacked while Rick sat in the big green chair, watching.

"I feel so guilty for not helping," he said again.

"Don't feel guilty, hon," I said, on my umpteenth trip in, arms loaded. "I'm happy to do this."

Tomorrow we'll celebrate our thirty-first anniversary. Tonight he gave me a card with an ape on the front, holding a bouquet of flowers. The message reads: "To my Darling Wife ... I got you a card that's just like me."

But I couldn't open the card. Flipping it over, I read, on the back: "It doesn't do what it's supposed to either! Happy Anniversary!"

I laughed. "But why are you giving me this tonight?"

"Because I don't know if I'll remember tomorrow."

Tuesday, August 21
Tranquil Acres, p.m.

Rick didn't do well last night: He trembled and sweated profusely all night. He got up for breakfast but immediately went back to bed. Things didn't improve during the day.

Tonight I sit quietly with only the cottage lamp on. I have a sense of foreboding about Rick's condition. His fever isn't coming down, he shuffles like a Parkinson's patient, and he hurts all over.

I gave him a full body massage a while ago. He groaned; said it felt good. But he can barely use that left arm, and when he sleeps, his eyelids remain open an eerie crack. Sometimes his eyeballs roll backward. Whatever this infection is, I don't like it. I'm taking him back to town first thing in the morning.

Wednesday, August 22
Midnight, back home

In retrospect, we shouldn't have gone to the lake at all. I'm back home. Rick is in the hospital, halfway across town.

All last night he twitched in bed. This morning he vomited when he stood up — and he could barely stand. The headache hadn't gone away and seemed even more vicious. I had to help him to the car.

Once at the hospital, Rick barely managed, with my assistance, to get out of the car. We limped in, carrying our bucket. I noticed the sign, "If you have vomiting or diarrhea, report it immediately."

"We have vomiting and diarrhea," I shouted.

A white-haired woman rushed out from behind the desk to lead us to triage.

"They have vomiting and diarrhea," she echoed, almost as loudly.

The triage nurse opened the door immediately and ushered Rick in, replacing our yellow ice-cream bucket with a stainless steel kidney basin.

Then she took his blood pressure (normal) and temperature (high) and led us into the same room we had waited in on Saturday. Rick did what he did on Saturday: got up on the bed and tried to sleep.

This time I did more praying than worrying.

When Jan arrived, he seemed alarmed by Rick's downward turn.

"I'm sending for a West Nile test, but the results will take several days," he said.

He performed a lumbar puncture (spinal tap) immediately. Rick sat, hunched over a table at the side of the bed, head in hands, face screwed up grotesquely as Jan painted his back burgundy, then stuck a needle in that looked about a foot long.

I recall thinking that the pain both in his head and throughout his body would kill him if they didn't do something for him soon.

After lumbar puncture, a patient must stay prone for the next several hours. They've admitted him for now, and they've also placed him in isolation until they find out what's making him so sick.

Jan has ordered a barrage of antibiotics to try to counter whatever this is. They're all connected to the same IV in Rick's hand. He keeps scratching at it.

Jan has also given an early diagnosis: meningitis, probably caused by West Nile virus. I would like to snatch Rick back from this place that has swallowed us both and speed back to Tranquil Acres, where the sky is blue and the water calm and no nurses or lab techs or doctors poke about.

I've always told our children, Anthony and Amanda, "Never set your foot on a road if you don't want to go where it leads." I don't like this road, but something in me tells me our only choice is to walk to the end of it.

Amanda must have called her brother. He phoned tonight and offered to come. How I'd love to have him here. But it's tourist season, a bad time for him to leave the little restaurant he manages in the mountains of British Columbia.

"Stay there, Anthony," I told him. "Wait until we know more."

Amanda, bless her heart, left the children with Daddy Kendall, drove to Tranquil Acres, packed up all our belongings, and dropped them off at our home. She can't even come into the hospital room to see her dad because of the possible danger to our littlest grandbean, still cozy in her womb. She stood in the doorway, though, and told him that she loved him.

Rick slept a good part of the day — between episodes of pain and fever and the vampire attacks, that is. I thought the lab techs and nurses would never stop poking about, inserting needles and taking blood.

Between his sleeps, he groaned much and talked little. When he did speak, he seemed not to understand his situation or know where he was, though he seemed to recognize, and even spoke to, those who popped in for a few seconds. All day he sweated terribly, like a swimmer freshly emerged from water. We had to change his sheets and gown at least a dozen times.

I contemplated staying all night but left at about 11:30. He seemed to be sleeping comfortably.

Thursday, August 23
E-mail Update

7:45 a.m.

Hi, Friends,

Sorry for the blanket e-mail. It's the easiest way to tell you that Rick isn't well. He has been having symptoms of West Nile disease, and until we know for sure what else this is, he's been placed in isolation, meaning even I have to don gown, mask, etc., to go in and see him.

When I left him last night, he was resting fairly comfortably, a relief after days of pain, even if it took morphine. I've just called the hospital, and they tell me he had a good night overall.

Yesterday morning, as we waited (and waited and waited) in

emergency for word on some kind of diagnosis, I sat reading one of my friend Grace Fox's books, *Moving from Fear to Freedom*. A statement jumped off the page. I can't quote it exactly, but it dealt with the importance of shifting our focus from the giants in the land to the God who promised to be with us in that land.

God had timed my reading of that chapter with precision. Whatever difficulties (or not!) the days ahead hold, I have decided to focus more on the fact — the marvel — that the God of the universe has promised to walk with us through them.

Thanks so much for praying.

Love,
Kathleen

P.S. Wear repellent.

Thursday August 23
Midnight

I'm writing this from a couch in the patients' lounge in ICU. I'll spend the night here.

Rick got progressively worse today. As the day ground on, it became clear that he needed more attention and monitoring. He's still in isolation.

Even while he slept today, his eyes remained open, or half open, sometimes rolling back. All day the pain in all his joints and muscles seemed unbearable and for most of the day sweat sheathed his body, glistening on his skin. Strangely, it smelled like a swimming pool change room.

I divided my time between wiping him down, giving him ice water, and changing his gown, helped by the nurses when they had time. He groaned almost constantly and sometimes didn't know where he was.

The worst moment came about midafternoon, when he grabbed one of the bedrails and lifted himself up slightly off the bed ...

SUNNY SIDE UP
March 20, 2008

There's a lot I would rather forget about the first month after the pirates of West Nile assaulted my husband. And there's plenty, thank God, the Preacher doesn't have to forget — he simply can't remember. Pain, high fever, and confusion made sure of that.

One memory I'll hold forever, though. On purpose. Because it's terrible. Because it's wonderful.

On his second day in hospital, the Preacher, wild-eyed and a-glistening with sweat, grabbed one of the bedrails with his only good arm and attempted to rise. He couldn't.

Fiercely, he glared. Loudly, he cried: "I can't, I can't ... I don't know who I am. Tell me my name. What's my name?"

I jumped from my chair beside his bed and grabbed his flailing hand.

"Richard Kenneth Gibson," I said.

Clinging to me, he repeated it slowly, like an obedient child: "Richard Kenneth Gibson." His head sank onto the pillow, but a second later the wild look returned. Up he came again, frantic.

"And then what?"

I didn't know how to answer. "What do you mean?"

"What comes next?"

His eyes, his eyes ... I had never seen them so lost, so bewildered. I thought fast. Help, Lord.

"Child of God."

He relaxed then. "Richard Kenneth Gibson, Child of God."

"And he loves you," I said.

"And he loves you," he repeated, as if reciting vows in a wedding service.

"I love you, too. Guess who else loves you?"

Not for a nanosecond did he hesitate. "Jesus." Then, in a thin, reedy voice, he began singing:

Jesus loves me! This I know,
For the Bible tells me so.

It didn't matter that staff hovered nearby. I joined him.

Little ones to Him belong,
They are weak, but He is strong.
Yes, Jesus loves me!
Yes, Jesus loves me!
Yes, Jesus loves me!
The Bible tells me so!

He fixed his eyes on mine, and our duet continued:

Jesus loves me! He who died,
Heaven's gate to open wide;
He will wash away my sin,
Let His little child come in.

Impassioned, he continued, "*Yes*, Jesus loves me. *Yes*, Jesus loves me, the Bible tells me so."

So there it was, then. The one true thing the pirates couldn't touch. A knowledge entrenched more deeply than fifty-four years of hearing his own name, repeated multiple times daily: Jesus loves me. Jesus died to take away my sins. Heaven is a real place and I am welcome there. Because the Bible tells me so.

The pirates robbed the Preacher of much. But they couldn't take his faith, or his song.

August 23 (continued)

... His muscles seemed hard and knotted, like a new rope. He grabbed my hand and held it. And held it and held it. I stood, realizing afresh the fragility of the precious things we take for granted.

A hand seeking ours. A quick peck on the cheek. The meeting of two pairs of loving eyes.

I haven't held his hand half enough over the thirty-one years we've been married. We should have taken more walks together, worked side by side and hand in hand more often.

━

Several pastors came and prayed with him today, including our friend Jim, the hospital chaplain.

Rick couldn't recall his own name today, but he seemed to know who people were the minute they came into the room. He even recognized Benjamin in the doorway, in Kendall's arms.

"Hi, Benjamin," he said, a little sun on his face for the first time.

But Benjamin was worried. He wanted to get down and go over to the bed, and didn't like being told that he couldn't.

"Gampa wary kick. *Wary* kick," he said later.

━

Jan has called in a specialist. Definitely meningitis, was their conclusion. Possibly bacterial meningitis. The specialist prescribed several more types of antibiotics.

"In the absence of a diagnosis, we must bombard your husband with drugs to treat every possible bug," he said. "His condition is critical."

"Do you think he should be moved to ICU?" I asked.

He seemed shocked at my question. "Absolutely," he said. "The man deserves a chance."

"Critical." It was the first time anyone had used that word so far. But those words, "He deserves a chance," chilled me.

After the recommendation, the staff wasted no time in shipping him off the ward to ICU. Rick has no idea where he is, and, in all his pain, doesn't seem to care.

His room is full of equipment, most of it plugged into a tall tower in the corner of the room. Oxygen, IV poles, monitors for heart rate, blood pressure, oxygen — some of it similar to what was in the ward-room; the rest more sophisticated.

Arriving here was like finding a refuge in the storm. I told the nurse who was to care for him on the night shift that I would like to sleep here tonight. That I was concerned about my husband's mental state and wanted to be near him if he needed me.

She told me I could sleep on the couch in the waiting room. Fetched me a pillow and blanket and a pitcher of water.

Thank God for kind people.

Friday, August 24
Evening

After yesterday's confusion, I didn't know what to expect when I walked into Rick's room this morning.

"Good morning, hon," I said.

"Hi," he responded a little slowly.

"Do you know your name today?"

"Rick Gibson."

"Good. And what do you do for a living?"

He thought on that one for several moments.

"Clergyman."

Since we've been in here, I've been reading him our daily six-pack (five Psalms and one chapter from the Proverbs). Every day there's been something that applies directly to our situation. I am awed and humbled by how relevant these ancient words are to us now. Sometimes as I read, I replace "enemies" with "diseases," and Rick's name for many of King David's personal pronouns.

I pray that this sinks deeply into his spirit, that all the years of immersing himself in God's Word will serve him well now.

Today his pain was less intense, thanks to morphine. He cooperated as much as he could with the staff, causing one to say, "We're so glad your husband is a gentle sort. The big ones usually get aggressive with this disease."

This disease. What disease? We're still not sure what we're fighting or why.

Chaplain Jim found me today, while I sat in the lounge as Rick slept. He asked all kinds of chaplain questions. I think my answers disappointed him. Long ago, I decided I must accept the bad in life as well as the good. That it's just a waste of energy and totally non-productive to wish things could be otherwise. God is with us in this dangerous place, so we are exactly where we are the safest.

God has been preparing me for this. I told Jim that. For a year or more, my spirit has sensed something dark on the horizon. I couldn't put my finger on why, but I felt certain my days as a pampered wife were dwindling to a trickle.

Perhaps this is the reason I often felt a strong urgency to be with my husband, a sadness each time we separated for even a day or two, a compulsion to buy a home of our own (parsonage life is nice, but it builds no equity), a desire to contribute more to the family income.

 ⌒

Jolene Cherland, a friend and the head of palliative care here, presented us today with a beautifully knit prayer shawl: soft as a cloud, in the colours of a sunny day at the sea. Women in her Lutheran church knit these for families in crisis, praying over each row for their encouragement, mercy, healing. It surrounds me as I write now: a tangible reminder of God's care. I will share it with Rick later.

 ⌒

Rick's bed looked short. His feet were rubbing against its foot.

"We either need to move you up in the bed or lengthen it," I said.

"Yes," he said, then thought a long while. "But there's another way." Each word was slow and measured. "Or we could ... let me think this through ... or we could ... *shorten me.*"

Good thing I was wearing a mask — he couldn't see me giggle. Or maybe he could.

"No ... hear me out. It would work. All you'd have to do is ... just cut an inch off my pants."

I giggled even harder, trying not to let him see, because his suggestion was so very serious.

He must have noticed, because he tried to hold up his hand.

"No, listen! I'm six one, right? So then I would only be six feet."

Later, seeing some nursing supplies on the corner of the cupboard, he pointed and asked the nurse what they were.

"Oh, that's just junk," she said.

"Junk," he repeated slowly as though examining a problem from every angle. "Oh."

Then: "Well, what I would like to know ... Can you tell me ... Is there enough to go all the way?"

"Enough what?" the nurse asked.

"Enough junk."

He hasn't been eating but did agree to try some cheese soup. I spooned it into his mouth, slowly at first, then spilled some on his sheets and apologized.

"That's because you're taking too long to get it into my mouth," he said.

So I went a little faster. Suddenly I felt him bumping my arm.

"If I didn't do that, you'd just keep shovelling it in, faster and faster," he said.

Oops.

He has difficulty with hospital food (I do, too), so I brought him some veggies from home. When I showed him cut-up bits of celery, cauliflower, and broccoli, he didn't know what they were, and couldn't choose. I held each one up and named them. Then he repeated the names after me, like a child, only he didn't get them quite right.

"Celly, foffoli." He gave up on the cauliflower. Then, his eyes large and curious like a child's, he said, "Is it always going to be like this?"

Thinking he meant his condition, I began to answer, "No, your brain is just finding its way back again."

He brushed me aside, with slow measured words. "No, no. What I want to know is, will there always be celery?"

This time he got the word right.

Will there always be celery? As long as our little boat floats, I'll give the man celery if he wants it. He always does. It's far and away his favourite raw veggie.

Friday, August 24
E-mail Update

Friends and Family,

I feel your prayers and support.

Doctors and nurses have warned that the cognitive difficulties may come and go — perhaps for weeks. Yesterday was full of those, but this morning Rick not only knew his name; he also knew mine.

"What's my name?" I asked.

He looked me over carefully with eyes that actually seemed to indicate there was something inside there.

"George," he said. Then, with the suggestion of a grin, "Kathleen."

The next thing he said — typical for Rick — was (a little belligerently), "Why are you asking me all these questions?"

The nurse answered that one. "Because you've been very sick, and we're testing the activity of your brain."

Our daily six-pack this morning was full of strengthening words, and I read them aloud to Rick. I am positive that with God's hand in ours, our dry valley eventually will be a place of springs, just as we read today in Psalm 84:6.

The highlight for Rick today came in the form of a visit from a person he called "my boss": Dr. Danny Gales, the former superintendent of our denomination's churches in this area. Dr. Gales prayed and read scripture. Tears flowed as the beautiful words of Psalm 91 filled our hearts and that ICU room.

Rick is the chairman of the city's evangelical ministerial, and several pastors arrived at the same time to visit him today. But other than my request for Dr. Gales's visit, no visitors were allowed in. Instead there was a short and rather ecumenical prayer meeting in the ICU family lounge. One guy was sitting there waiting for someone else. I'm sure he had no idea what awaited him when he stepped in earlier.

I laughed often today over some of Rick's crazy confusion. After he called me George this morning when I asked him my name, I tested him again during lunch.

"That's good stuff," I said, as I fed him chocolate pudding. "Your wife should make it for you sometimes."

"She does, every now and then," he said.

"What's her name?"

"Now and then," he said. Definite grin this time.

The synapses are trying to connect. All his vital signs are good tonight, and his pain is down.

The nurses are finding it difficult finding adequate veins for IVs. They keep collapsing, because of his low blood pressure, I assume. Please pray for good veins tomorrow.

Pray also for three other patients in ICU with the same problem as Rick's. Until this meningitis is confirmed to be a result of West Nile, this is what one medical staff member calls "an alarming mystery."

Thanks so much.

Faith,
Kathleen

Saturday, August 25
9 p.m.

I've been here for twelve hours today. He's been sleeping, but has begun to thrash. I roll my chair over closer.

"What's the matter, hon?" I ask.

"I gotta go. I gotta go, or I'll sleep here all night."

"We want you to."

His right hand — he can't move the left one at all now — suddenly begins beating the rail.

"What are you doing?"

"I don't know how to get this down."

"Why do you want it down?"

"Because I have to get home! I have to get home!"

I remind him that he needs to stay here, that he's in the hospital fighting a very serious disease, and that it will take time.

He settles for a minute. Then says, as though his heart is breaking, "Let's go, hon. Let's go *now*. If we don't go now, I might never make it home."

On a card that I made him for our anniversary, I had included these words: "You are my human rock." Tonight I lay my head on that crumbling rock and cried, softly, so he wouldn't notice. It's the first time I've cried for us since we came in here.

But then I got my Bible out of the closet and read aloud some shepherd verses. I told Rick that God wants to pick him up in his arms and care for him like a shepherd cares for a wounded sheep, that it's his turn to be served now, and mine to give service, and that he'll have to help me with this role reversal. He's so much better at serving than I am.

He went back to sleep, then woke and said, "I'm finally realizing that I can't go home with you. You'd better go, hon, so I can get some sleep."

Saturday, August 25
E-mail Update

Friends and Family,

Today was better and worse. Rick did speak more, and didn't have to think quite so hard about how to form the words. His veins also seemed to support the needles better. We praise God. Thanks so much for praying.

His heart rate went lower and lower all day, ending up in the thirties frequently. Every time it did, it set off a red light and an alarm. Not low enough to need any kind of intervention, apparently — the ICU nurses weren't terribly concerned.

He gave me one good chuckle today.

He let out a long, loud moan when I thought he was sleeping.

"What is it?" I asked.

"Nothing. I just had to make a noise. It's too quiet in here."

Actually, it's not quiet. Monitors and medical machines click constantly and an air conditioner motor hums (yesterday he insisted there was a train in the room). It only seems quiet because one of the side effects of his condition has been the deterioration of his already diminished hearing. Whether this will be permanent, I don't know.

I told him we were going to need sign-language classes to communicate soon.

"You've been suggesting that for years," he said.

He's right. I praised God for this indication that his fabulous memory is returning.

He has suffered damage to the muscles on his left side, particularly his arm. That too may be only temporary. He can move his other limbs, but he can't yet turn over, stand, or sit by himself, or even feed himself. In most cases of West Nile, we're told, this gets better.

He was frustrated today, anxious to be up "doing stuff" (his words). The hardest part of the day was when he begged to go home. Several times I told him we couldn't, carefully explaining why. He couldn't comprehend that.

"Hon, if we don't go *now*, I might never make it home," he said again.

Tonight I tried to get his specialist to give me an idea of the long-term effects of this illness. That's when he told me that he believes Rick actually has bacterial (hence the isolation and gowning, masks, gloves) meningitis and encephalitis. He said he wasn't certain that it was caused by West Nile.

"This disease causes permanent damage, even death," he said.

I believe him about the seriousness of this condition, but I refuse to despair. He doesn't know about the mighty team of prayer warriors across the globe. My prayer is simply that God's will be done in Rick's body and our lives in the days ahead.

Thanks again, *everyone*, for praying. God allowed this and will see us through it as we continue to trust. I can't say I don't worry about the days ahead for our ministry, but I'm trying hard to remain focused on one day at a time. We've both taken considerable comfort from the Word as I read it aloud in his room.

Benjamin and Tabatha are missing Gampa, Amanda says, and she would love to see her dad, too. Tomorrow morning I'm going to walk around the hospital grounds to see if there's a way to access the window of his ground floor ICU room. No, I'm not going to help them break in, but Rick may be cheered by seeing their bright faces through "the looking glass."

That reminds me of something written by the Apostle Paul: "Now we see but a poor reflection, as in a mirror, but then we shall see face to face. Now I know in part; then I shall know fully even as I am fully known" (1 Corinthians 13:12).

This is the best part of today for me: being reminded that for all who know Christ, the looking glass will disappear one day and we'll be able to march right past all the hard stuff we don't understand, the perplexing mysteries we each face, and touch the face of the only one in the universe who knows the answers.

Faith,
Kathleen

Sunday, August 26

The virus, it seems, is still worming its way deeper into his brain. He seems to have retreated behind a blank stare of an almost Parkinson's-like state when he's not sleeping: eyes large, fixed forward, not blinking.

"Are you processing, hon?" I asked him.

The answer came back in a slow nod. Nods are more frequent than words. Once he nodded about fifteen times in answer to something, slowly, as though thinking very carefully.

Sunday, August 26
E-mail Update

Friends and Family,

I knew something was different the moment I walked into the ICU unit this morning. The bank of gowns, masks, and gloves was missing from outside Rick's door.

"The test came back," his nurse told me. "Positive for West Nile. As we suspected."

Knowing a definite cause of this meningoencephalitis somehow makes things clearer, though not any easier. Rick has sustained considerable muscular and neurological damage, and all of that will take time to rebuild.

Physiotherapists will begin working with him tomorrow, the nurses told me tonight.

Today I told him when and where the timeline seems right for The Bite to have occurred: possibly at the Teddy Bear Picnic for the church youngsters the week prior to when his symptoms began.

"I guess when it happened isn't as important as what will happen," he said slowly.

He's right. Hindsight makes experts of us all. But I was heartened by his brief comment — one of the few he made today — because it indicated that his brain is beginning to grab hold once again of the concept of time.

He asked only once today where he was and why. And he slept a lot and ate little. His heart rate was in the high forties, low fifties — an improvement over yesterday's alarming lows.

It was the Lord's Day today. We celebrated by reading scripture and singing hymns. Bracing hymns that spoke about our healing God. Though he couldn't join in, emotions swept across his face, particularly during one of his favourite choruses that speaks of God making a way where there seems to be no way, and working in ways we cannot see.

We both believe that. But his specialist told me again tonight that Rick's case is a critical one. That in cases this severe there's a ten percent mortality rate. Wow! As Amanda pointed out, this means a ninety percent chance of recovery. Add to that the tremendous army of people across Canada and on four continents who are praying and I would say we're up over a one-hundred-percent chance. God's healing power is at work, without a doubt.

The big concern today: that side effects won't creep in, pneumonia and blood clots specifically. We'd be so grateful if you'd pray about this, as well as that Rick's neurological damage will be minimal and his recovery complete.

Faith, faith,
Kathleen

Monday, August 27

The fluid buildup in Rick's chest bothers me. Today I tried to help by pounding on his chest. While thumping away, I heard a commotion at the nursing station. Whatever the nurses had seen on their monitors, it had caused quite a kerfuffle.

"That's bed one!" someone shouted. They all flocked to Rick's room — and found me pounding on said patient's chest. I had inadvertently set off every beeper, bell, and alarm possible.

"Know what the hardest thing about this is?" asked the man on that bed, later.

"What's that?"

"The emotion."

I waited for an explanation.

"Knowing what I could do, and what I can't do now."

His brain, taxed by the virus, was frantically attempting to come to grips with reality.

"Hon, I wish I could help. But I think for now there's going to be a new normal."

He nodded slowly.

⟋

A sweetheart of a physiotherapist entered our lives today. Melissa tried to assess his needs by having him move everything that's moveable. Fingers, hand, wrist, ankles, knees, toes. He grimaced often, but obeyed well.

I cried, watching. The enormity of what it will take to rebuild Rick slammed me against this hard truth: My days of dependence on this man are over.

Like Peter, Peter, Pumpkin Eater's wife, I've been a kept wife all our marriage.

Rick and I have often laughed at the way we work. For the most part he likes being "oot and aboot" and active. I like being home, alone and still, and writing.

As for grocery shopping, I make lists sometimes, but he does most of it. He does the driving when we're together. He makes most of the big decisions. He lugs in the salt for the water softener. He mows the lawn and blows the snow. He takes out the garbage. He fills up the car with gas and gets it fixed. He changes the cat litter, most often. He barbecues. He does laundry, too.

And he buys me flowers.

It's true, and I've always known it: I don't deserve him.

But the biggest thing is that Rick likes working with money. I would prefer to use marbles or beads or rocks. Anything but paper and metal — or even plastic with numbers on it.

As far as I'm concerned, money is an occupational hazard.

In the next weeks, I'm going to have to learn Gibson Finances 101, all the ins and outs. But if I think my learning curve will be steep, his will be steeper. To sit back and watch me make the big decisions may be a greater hazard to his life than this virus.

But with God's help, and a little help from my friends, we will make these changes, and it will improve our health all round.

⌒

Benjamin cried himself blue today. He desperately wanted to come in and see his Gampa, but so far I'm still the only family member allowed into this sanctum of bodily restoration.

However, the nurse allowed his entire family to step inside for just a brief moment ... to watch him sleep.

And they stood over the bed where the man of God lay.

Tabatha stretched out her arms, and Benjamin, tucked close against his daddy's chest, looked the man on the bed over carefully.

"Gampa seeping. Gampa wary kick. Gampa weally kick!"

"Yes, we have to pray for Gampa," his mama said.

Immediately the Bean bowed his head, clasped his hands, and said in a hushed voice: "Deah Jesus, please make Gampa better. Amen."

I told Rick all that later. His face registered nothing, but his shoulders started shaking.

Tuesday, August 28

Today I rolled his reclining Broda chair into a position to where he could see the view out the window: four barely swaying evergreen tops and a tall gray smokestack topped with a black lid, supported by four black sticks. And white clouds unbroken except for blue sky in the shape of a capital F.

"Hey, hon, look, there's a world out there!" I said.

He nodded slowly and shut his eyes.

One of the nurses called me out of the room.

"It's very important not to give too much stimulation to a patient with a brain injury, and that's what this disease is," she told me carefully. "The brain needs lots of time to rebuild what has been lost."

Suddenly it was all too much. Noticing that I was teetering on the brink of a small meltdown, she put her hand on my arm and led me over to a window in a quiet alcove where she gently educated me on the art of nursing those with brain injuries.

With encephalitis, she explained, the spinal fluid exerts tremendous pressure on the brain. Patients need long periods of quiet to allow the brain to heal. In wakeful times, gentle stimulation is necessary to begin rebuilding what has been lost, but over-stimulation only brings about anxiety and distress.

The kindness of our friends overwhelms me. We have received more cards and e-mails than I can count. Care packages, gifts, fruit baskets, flowers, books, phone calls.

Chicken soup with dumplings awaited me on the doorstep tonight. From Kay and Gene Kuemper, next door. I stood at the counter and ate it from the plastic tub. Divine, but there are some things even chicken soup can't heal.

Tuesday, August 28
E-mail Update

Friends and Family,

In our six-pack today, we found this, from Psalm 118:17: "I will not die but live, and will proclaim what the LORD has done." I'm standing on that one. We believe God is answering your prayers for Rick's healing, and we praise him for every small step.

Rick had a spectacular day. He ate seven bites of food, drank three cups of V8 juice (he hasn't eaten for days), had a great poop (that's *huge* for most ICU patients), sat up supported in the chair for hours (not without immense pain and complaining), responded well to the physiotherapist (even though she asked him to do silly things like "bend your fingers and toes"), and smiled and managed to high-five Benjamin when we snuck him in to bring Gampa the home-cooked meal his mama made, to entice him to eat more. (Didn't work.)

His heart rate is low again. His chest X-ray showed a fluid buildup around his lungs. And he had two panic attacks. In spite of those things, today was still the best day by far.

The nurses remind me that it's a roller-coaster journey and that tomorrow the cart may plunge again, but before I left my husband's bedside we thanked God for this wonderful, fabulous, very good, lovely, quiet day.

Please keep praying whenever God reminds. We thank you from our toenail-tips up.

Love,
Kathleen

SUNNY SIDE UP
August 29

Find the Right Rock to Build On

Today I read Psalm 11, where King David of Israel recalls that when his enemies pursued him, his fraidy-cat acquaintances, sure of defeat, recommended that he flee to the mountains.

"When the foundations are being destroyed," they ask, "what can the righteous do?"

I love the king's answer (Gibson paraphrase): "The Lord knows what's going down! He'll deal with it. Stay cool, people!"

Psalm 71 eavesdrops on one of David's conversations with God. "You are my rock and my fortress ... my strong refuge," he says. In verse 20, he adds, "You will restore my life again; from the depths of the earth you will again bring me up!"

No matter how devastating life's blows, and David experienced many, he had learned that only one true thing would always remain: God, his rock of refuge. He had also learned the futility of building a life around anything but the trustworthy character of God.

"You are my human rock." Only days ago, I wrote those words in a homemade thirty-first anniversary card to the Preacher.

I couldn't know that within the week I would be penning this column in the intensive care unit of our local hospital, watching him struggle with meningitis and encephalitis, results of his critical case of West Nile.

A virtually weightless enemy has crumpled my rock. For a time.

Plenty of things go through one's head when one is confronted with an enemy. Like David's friends, I long to flee for the mountains — to those of my B.C. upbringing, where pine and fir whispered, where rain fell in a benedictive caress, where my problems dropped beside the trail like so much dead bark.

But I want to go there only if the Preacher can go with me, and therein lies the problem. We won't be hiking for a while. The Preacher is too busy with other things at the moment. Like remembering his own name, and mine, and where he is and why. And learning all over again how to sit up, feed himself, walk. And understanding why he can't go home with me at the end of the day.

In the middle of all this, I remember how important it will be for the Preacher and me, in the valley ahead, to find shelter in David's Rock. Not Rick the Rock, as people sometimes refer to the Preacher, but the Divine Rock, who has proved over and over to us that he is a trustworthy God.

And unlike our frail human bodies, this rock won't crumble.

Thursday, August 30

According to the written employment agreements, the church will pay Rick's salary, minus car allowance, for four months. After that, our disability insurance will kick in: $1,250 a month.

"Can you live on that?" asked Dr. Larry Dahl, a long-time friend and colleague in ministry, and now our denominational district superintendent.

"Absolutely not," I answered. "I'm a financial imbecile, but even I know how much it costs to live these days. And I won't have time to write again for a while, it seems."

As I drove back to the hospital after that breakfast meeting with Larry, I kept seeing the same poster — an advertisement for an upcoming local play — on billboards, on signs, even at the hospital in the stairwells. It showed a woman tilted, as though bracing for a topple. "Help Me, I'm Falling," it read.

The irony didn't escape me.

But when I kissed Rick goodnight, I thanked God for this opportunity to experience him in a new way. As I walked home, the sky was clear, the air fragrant with waning summer scents: harvest, BBQ, freshly mowed grass. As long as I can see a patch of blue and smell sweet country air, I have reason to be grateful.

Friday, August 31

When I got to Rick's room today, he commanded me almost immediately to move his legs. This is something new, and it fills me with the hope that what wants to move, will be restored.

So I sit or hunch over him and shake, rub, bend, scratch, pound, jiggle — do whatever I can to coax life into his useless, paralyzed limbs.

I noticed that today they had more strength than yesterday. While sitting up in the chair, Rick brought his knees slightly toward each other, and when I lifted his ankle and told him to raise his foot, he did that, too, slightly.

FROM A PREVIOUSLY UNPUBLISHED ARTICLE, WRITTEN IN SEPTEMBER 2007

Beauty from Brokenness

I spotted a birdbath at an artist friend's studio a few weeks ago — and knew I must have it.

Sonja Pawliw crafts exquisite mosaics from glass and broken china dishes. The birdbath was one of them.

Stepping-stones, garden balls, chairs, tables ... all Sonja needs is a surface: a clay pot, a dented garbage can, an old tin, a watering jug, a coffee table, rickety chairs.

No matter how worthless her materials may be, Sonja makes them breathtaking, and often functional again.

Mosaics have always intrigued me, and so has old china. Only hours before spotting the birdbath, I had begun making a mosaic from broken china myself. My friend Judy joined me.

As we worked quietly, choosing our scheme and gluing broken pieces onto cement stepping-stone bases, I explained why I appreciate mosaics so much.

"Imagine all these shattered plates and cups," I said. "Useless and good for nothing but the trash heap, and here we are making them into something beautiful. Isn't it amazing?"

Judy was quiet for a moment. Then she said, "Not only something beautiful, but something entirely new."

I reflected on her words as I searched for just the right shade of yellow plate chip to contrast with the blue border around my stepping-stone's edge. In the centre I had placed an antique 1930s Bavarian plate, white with a cluster of glorious pink roses.

The plate had been a favourite for a long time. When it fell off my cupboard I saved the pieces, hoping to glue it back together some day.

On the day Judy and I began our stepping-stones, we discovered that we had purchased the wrong kind of grout to fill the spaces between the china pieces. We dashed into town.

I rarely see Sonja, but on our way into the store we met her coming out. I laughed and explained what we'd been doing. Always hospitable, she invited us to her home for a quick look at her mosaics and renowned gardens.

And that's where I spotted the birdbath, in Sonja's small shop beside her garage studio. A tall column of chips and shatters from a hundred different pieces of china, with blue marbles embedded around the rim of the bowl.

It actually made my heart skip a beat.

"Sonja, would you please save that birdbath for me?" I said finally. "I think it's the most wonderful piece here, and I want to buy it."

She agreed. I told her I couldn't pay for several weeks.

Before I returned, though, a split-second occurrence changed my life — perhaps forever. My husband (my pillar) was bitten by a mosquito and has contracted West Nile neurological disease. As I write, he lies in an ICU bed, paralyzed in a good part of his body and struggling with mental confusion.

In this strange wild place to which we have been ushered, material things, however lovely, mean almost nothing. I didn't even remember the birdbath until weeks later. How foolish, I thought. How shallow is a woman who becomes smitten by a birdbath? But I had spoken for it and felt compelled to pick it up.

Leaving my husband sleeping in his ICU bed, I drove to Sonja's studio. Not until I saw the birdbath again, this time adorned with a large SOLD sign, did I realize why God had endeared it so much to me several weeks earlier.

Before me I saw a strong pillar lovingly fashioned from brokenness alone. And not only were the china pieces still exquisite, they were now part of something entirely new: a bowl of blessing to water others. The birdbath now symbolized the faith and hope I must maintain for my husband — that God would do the same with his broken body.

I stood, overwhelmed, and all the more so for Sonja's comment.

"That birdbath comes from a very special place," she said quietly. "Under all the china pieces is a washstand that came from the rectory beside my church."

Friday, August 31
E-mail Update

Dear Family and Friends,

Rick is making slow progress. He has feeling in his legs and his left arm, but they remain non-functional. His right side is somewhat stronger, though still very weak. He is able to pass a few forks of food into his mouth before tiring too much to continue. He talks in complete sentences — though very short ones and only occasionally.

Yesterday evening, for the first time since we came here eleven days ago, he used a very important word for the first time.

The nurse asked him if our arrangements of the multitude of pillows we prop around him each night was comfortable.

"Comfortable," he said.

It seemed a huge step. Nothing about this condition is comfortable, and he is weary.

In fact, he was already tired going into this. We were only a day into our vacation when we returned and he was admitted. We've been going to the same lakeside cottage every year lately, and he always sleeps the first week, so he was programmed to sleep during this time.

The worst of the crisis has passed, and I anticipate that he will soon be moved into a regular ward, where he should be able to receive a few more visits. His mother, Gerry, has travelled out from Ontario. It's so lovely to come home to someone other than Moses the cat.

The other evening, as I massaged Rick's legs, I began singing a favourite old hymn:

Day by day, and with each passing moment,
Strength I find to meet my trials here ...

As I rubbed, another voice joined in, reedy and very crackly:

Trusting in my Father's wise bestowment,
I've no cause for worry or for fear.

Rick. Singing. His spirit is making the divine connection. And I thanked God for that, too.

Please pray for the healing not only of his body, but also of his will and emotions — for a fighting spirit and restoration of hope. He's had a huge loss and is trying to process all this. We know all of you have busy lives, and many of you are going through crises of your own. We don't want this to be an added burden; just pray for continued strength as God reminds you, and know that we, like you, are held forever,

In His Fantastic Grip,
Kathleen and Rick

Saturday, September 1

The "overwhelm-ment" continues. I am overwhelmed by people's kindness. Overwhelmed by all the financial details I have to work out. Overwhelmed by the consequences of this disease. Overwhelmed by how much I have to do now. And yet, strangely, at peace. We are in good hands. Kind hands. God's hands.

A nurse took me aside today.

"We've noticed that your husband has no, uh, affirmation for those caring for him," she said. "We find it strange, considering his profession. Is he always like this?"

Generally Rick is caring and considerate, but he's not an effusive man. And though it's true I've sometimes had to coach him to say thank you, the man I've seen in the last eleven days is not the man I've known and loved.

He doesn't know what he wants when we ask him. He takes forever to answer, and if we grow impatient or ask again, he says, rather tartly, "I'm thinking." If I ask him how he feels about something, he says, "I don't know how I feel, or what I should be feeling." The disease has stolen his opinions and his emotions.

When I told the nurse this, she said she had thought as much and explained that personality changes are one of the effects of encephalitis.

As gently as I could, I told Rick how important it is for him to exercise his emotional and mental muscles, and to begin by smiling and saying thank you to his nurses. By the end of the shift he was doing that, in a whispered, rote sort of way, much to their surprise.

Sunday, September 2

When I walked onto the ward this morning, a nurse greeted me cheerfully with the news: "Today is moving day!"

Rick has graduated from ICU to a regular ward. This is supposed to be a good thing.

This afternoon, while Mom came up to sit with Rick ("You get some rest," she said), I went home and researched West Nile neurological disease — the first chance I've had to do so.

What I read alarmed me. West Nile is a far more serious disease than anyone guessed. Or perhaps I'm the only babe in the mosquito-ridden woods.

One of the first verses that God brought to my attention during my daily reading of our six-packs talked about how he strengthened King David's arms for battle and his fingers for war. I wondered why. Tonight I think I know part of the reason.

Jan, our friend and doctor, has moved two provinces over. I already miss him. Until his replacement arrives, several other doctors will care for his patients. One entered the room today, and asked, "How are you today?"

Rick, his eyes shut to the pain and confusion, said nothing.

"We've had better days," I said.

The doctor turned my way.

"Would you please leave the room?" he said.

Dumbfounded, I started for the door. Then rethought, hesitated, turned, and said, "Actually, I prefer to stay while you examine my husband."

"And I prefer you to leave," he said.

We went back and forth until he finally said, "I won't examine your husband unless you leave."

Still in shock, I stood in the hall, fuming. When he finally let me back in — a good ten minutes later — he said, "Do you have any questions?"

"Yes, I do. My first question is why did you ask me to leave?"

"I never assess a patient with anyone else in the room," he said. "Is there anything else?"

"Yes," I said. "That will not happen again. I won't leave the room again while you examine my husband."

"You must. I will not examine him otherwise. This is my policy."

"Then you will not examine him again. That is my policy."

"Fine."

I couldn't believe we were having this discussion, and in the civil tones we were both maintaining.

"Would you please refer him to Wascana Rehabilitation Centre in Regina?" I asked.

He agreed to make the referral at his first opportunity.

I did ask for the results of his assessment. He said it seemed the virus has done all the damage it would do, and that from now on Rick's body would begin a tedious road to recovery.

All tallied, Rick is much worse today than yesterday. Lord, help my temper not to get in the way of good care for Rick, my husband.

Tuesday, September 4
E-mail Update

Hi, Friends and Family,

Rumours are flying around town that Rick is better. Here's the truth: The body pirates, as I've come to call this disease, have taken their plunder, leaving us with the mop-up operations — assessing what remains and rebuilding, with God's help, both ship and contents.

Rick still can't sit, stand, or move his left arm. In many respects, he is a paralyzed man, and it will be some time, and take considerable work, before that changes and we return to our real life — or the new normal.

I'm immensely grateful, though, for what the pirates have left behind. Rick's words, though they come slowly and only after much thought, show that he's completely cognizant. I missed his magnificent mind dreadfully during the days it was lost to me.

West Nile neurological disease is a complicated disease of the central nervous system. In my research, I have repeatedly read and am finally beginning to understand that there are no quick fixes when it hits as severely as it has hit Rick.

Of course, we'd prefer an instantaneous healing, and God knows that. But for his own reasons, the one who makes our bodies and souls often chooses a different route to wholeness.

Rick and I accept that, and are eager to learn what he will teach us through it.

Now we play hurry up and wait. The doctor caring for him has recommended a transfer to Wascana Rehabilitation Centre in Regina, two hours south of Yorkton. Wascana is one of Canada's finest rehab centres. Our hospital isn't able to provide the specialized care he will need in the days ahead, and we pray for a bed to open soon.

Meanwhile, Rick's joint pain has increased steadily since the week-end, and he still has vicious headaches. Too much stimulation tires him out and sets back his progress, so visitors are still limited to primarily family, and except for Mom Gibson and me, even those for only a few minutes. This is to avoid both further infection and weariness.

Your stories of how God sustained and enabled you through

medical crises of your own have inspired us to remain bold, hope-filled, and prayerful. So do a few verses from Isaiah 41 that a friend reminded us of, the ones that say, "You are my servant ... I have *chosen* you. Don't sweat the hard stuff" (Gibson paraphrase, very sleepy edition).

Faith,
Kathleen

Wednesday, September 5

Rick has been transferred to commode and bath and Broda chair by means of several lifts. His favourite is the one I call the people crane, but sometimes the staff use the sit-to-stand lift, a contraption with a belt that goes around his middle and has channels for his knees. Once the belt is fastened, and his knees in place, the machine lifts him electronically.

He hates it. Because of his paralysis and weakness, he can't hold the handles or do the minimal standing the machine requires. Only the two male orderlies operate this machine correctly, he says. Despite his protests that he has no strength to assist the lift to do its job, some of the staff insist on using it.

Today during a transfer his legs collapsed and the belt slipped upward. He plunged downward, and both his arms flew upward, pushed there by the belt, which halted abruptly under his armpits.

Later, he had intense pain in his left shoulder, which worsened throughout the day, even though we treated it with ice packs.

A psychologist visited today.

"How are you doing?" he asked.

I had asked Rick that very thing when I came into his room this morning.

"Better," he surprised me by saying. But to this doctor, he said, "I can't do anything."

"That's not true," the doctor responded. "You can do a lot of things."

"It's no wonder people get depressed," the doctor told me later.

"They look at the things they can't do and keep their focus there. They work to change the unchangeable, and all it can do is frustrate. Instead, they should look at something they can do, anything they can change, however small, and work at increasing it. Maybe I can't run a marathon today, but I can run a mile, and maybe tomorrow I'll be able to run two."

SUNNY SIDE UP
September 12

On Rebuilding Rick

Melissa, the physiotherapist, comes in frequently to help the Preacher re-acquire the abilities West Nile disease has stolen.

Rebuilding Rick, I call it. He hates it.

"Let's do some knee bends," she says cheerfully.

"I can't," he shoots back, too readily.

"Try," she says. She puts one hand under his knee, places the other on the sole of his foot, and begins pushing. "Push back! Fight me, fight me! Don't let me do it, don't let me do it!"

I fix my eyes on his upper thigh and see a minute ripple disturb its surface when he squeezes his eyes shut and tries to obey.

"Holy Hannah, you're strong!" she says, encouraging him as a mother would a child.

The Preacher is a challenge for several reasons. Because he's large, for one, which makes his limbs very heavy and causes problems with some of the exercises. And because he's in such tremendous pain, for another.

But the disease itself — a recent arrival (1999) in North America — presents another obstacle. Medical professionals are still feeling their way, with only nine years of history and no long-term case studies of patients affected by severe West Nile disease to guide them.

"This disease manifests very much like polio," Melissa has told me several times, to help me understand.

I wish I had a magic key to release him from this prison. I wish I could fight for him, take the pain for him — or at least share it. But all I can do during these therapy sessions is sit in the corner and pray for relief. And fetch ice, and rub on liniment afterward.

Tonight, after I finished reading a passage from 1 John to him, I asked him, "Hon, do you ever ask God why this happened to you?"

He closed his eyes and the skin between his eyes creased like a folded towel. He does that when he's feeling strong emotion, I've noticed. This time he spoke through the wrinkles.

"It's never why," he whispered. "What I want to know is *how*? How is God going to get the glory through this?"

I ask the how question myself as well. Regularly. Daily. Sometimes hourly. And plead that we'll both be found worthy to bear this gift of pain.

Thursday, September 6

Everyone knows I hate numbers. Which is why it's so curious that I've been counting things, and without even thinking. The rows of bricks on the hospital wall across from our ICU window: thirty-one between each floor. And outside our wardroom: twenty-five. The ceiling panels in this room (fourteen, of various sizes), the number of seconds between clicks on the IV machine (six), the number of Rick's get well cards hanging on the wall and on the curtain rods (forty-eight and increasing daily).

I can only imagine that my mind is subconsciously searching for order in this chaos of wilderness where I find myself.

Friday, September 7

Hoping Rick will be transferred soon, I have left the doctor issue alone. The doctor does his rounds before I get here in the morning, or after I leave at night. We've been avoiding each other.

He came in early this evening, around nine. The light was out over Rick's bed and I had restful music playing. He walked toward the bed, then noticed me sitting in the corner. He backed away and turned to leave. I stopped him by holding out my hand.

"Doctor, I still won't leave, but I'm sorry we got off to such a bad start."

"I won't assess him tonight then," he said, a little surprised. "He looks as though he's sleeping anyway."

"Do you always assess him?"

"Not always."

We went on to have a cautiously pleasant chat about West Nile and its comparative illnesses — polio, for one — as well as its consequences for our society in the years ahead. Both of us felt our way around the conversation, groping for the bumps that cause pain, and surprisingly finding none. In spite of the rough start, maybe we'll get along after all.

Friday, September 7
E-mail Update

Family and Friends,

We are seeing small evidences daily of returning strength, but this process of rebuilding Rick is a little like watching a tree grow. His nerves have been damaged, and nerves are what tell the muscles to operate.

Nerves do have the ability to grow back, at 1 to 3 mm per day, I've read. However, no one knows exactly how far from the muscles Rick's nerves have suffered injury, so it's impossible to say how long this process will take.

To those who say we need to believe for a miracle, I say any amount of healing, no matter how speedy, is miraculous. We are truly fearfully and wonderfully made, and the fact that Rick has survived the pirates' attack is miraculous to begin with.

The truth is, none of us are getting out of here alive. *Something* will kill us all in the end, and for most of us it will be sickness and/or old age. The great end of this human story is, for the person who trusts

Jesus with every aspect of their life and death, that the long dark tunnel of human suffering is never hopeless. It always ends in glorious light. This isn't all there is, people.

Of course God can, if he chooses, heal instantaneously, and in this microwave age isn't that what we all want? But we'd have to be blind and ignorant not to realize that most of the time he chooses the slow route to returning our fragile bodies to health and strength.

If that's his will, we accept that, and trust that he's going to reveal himself to us in surprising, faith-strengthening ways. In fact, he already has.

Please pray for continued trust. We know that God holds both us and the end of this road securely in his control, but we are human and value the encouragement of others to dig deep and find the resolve to push past the physical, mental, emotional, and spiritual barriers this disease has caused.

It may be a while before a bed opens up in Wascana Rehabilitation Centre, the doctor says. Weeks? Months?

Meanwhile, we're going ahead ourselves, those of us caring for him through the day. Mom Gibson, Melissa the physiotherapist, and I regularly put Rick through his paces, moving his legs and arms to prevent atrophy and encourage the nerves to reconnect to the muscles. Some are already reconnecting. Praise God for that.

Though his legs can't bear his weight, Rick tells me that they go off walking all by themselves in the night — a signal that his system is raring to get back to work.

We're going to try something this week. I've daily seen improvements, both in Rick's physical health and his mental state. Though he still tires really quickly, he has agreed that he's ready for company: that he needs to see some of his friends and parishioners.

If you'd like to visit, please come, but plan to stay no longer than five minutes, and PLEASE, if you have any kind of bug, suspected or otherwise (especially a mosquito!), just stay home and pray.

Faith,
Kathleen

Saturday, September 8

He's been having horrible nights, calling frequently for the staff to shift him, much to the disgruntlement of some. He didn't even nap last night, he said. Just tossed and turned. Finally, around four, he had the nurses put him into the Broda chair.

"I like it when you read scripture," he said to me today. "I like hearing your voice."

The Word is feeding us both, as our bodies are stretched beyond their usual routines. "Please pass the Word," I want to say in weaker moments — that's how tangible a support it is to me. To Rick, too.

Tonight he broke down as I read from the epistles. Not loudly, and not overmuch, but I saw again that great heart of devotion and love for God's Word. How he must long to read it for himself, as he has done daily for so many years.

Sunday, September 9

He didn't sleep well last night. When I arrived at his bedside this morning, he told me about it, spilling it out like a child freshly home from school, reporting on a very bad day.

A few of the staff have been less than compassionate, he feels. Last night, someone chided him for going to sleep too soon, and for not socializing. (How does a paralyzed man in a private room socialize?) Some, it seems, believe his symptoms are psychosomatic. In the absence of education about West Nile, this isn't surprising.

This morning, as I read our six-pack aloud, I came to Psalm 69, the entirety of which seem to have been written especially for Rick. David pleads with God to remember his suffering, to rescue him from the deep waters of his trouble before he sinks, to answer him, to not hide his face from him.

Verse 20 moves even closer to our situation:

Scorn has broken my heart and has left me helpless; I looked for sympathy and there was none; for comforters, but I found none.

Our six-pack never disappoints — sometimes it even sets us up for
a laugh.

Rick hates the food here, and has no appetite. After I finished feeding him the other day, I noticed his medicine cup, still full of a pale-
coloured liquid, beside his plate. I put it up to his mouth. He drank
it obediently.

A second after he guzzled it down, his eyes popped wide open.

"That was *vinegar*," he said, highly offended.

Oil and vinegar, actually. The dressing for his salad came in the
same kind of medicine cup that holds one of his regular meds.

I recalled that incident today, when I came to verse 21 in Psalm 69:
"They put gall in my food, and gave me vinegar for my thirst."

I can't remember a better laugh.

Tuesday, September 11

Tabatha took five steps today, Kendall told me. Her first five steps. I'm
missing my grandbaby girl's first steps.

This afternoon, I came home, walked down to my office to check
the e-mails, and passed the room where the Beans sleep when they're
over. It was littered with their toys and small foldout Pooh couch. I
recalled Rick's excitement when he found it at Toys R Us. Suddenly I
felt it keenly, this great tear that has ripped me from my real life as
efficiently as a perforated tab on a page.

I sat with a young nurse the other night, one who could practice
a tad more compassion. I told her stories of Rick's life, explaining
what he's lost: mobility, profession, some memory, and so much
more. Before I finished, I saw tears in her eyes.

But until today I've never thought long and seriously about what
I have lost. Not only have the pirates stolen my real life and my real
husband. They've also made me lay aside the most precious little
people in the world to me.

I looked at their diaper-changing table, the little red wagon full of
toys, the mussed up desk, the watercolour paints lying upside down
on the floor, and realized that somewhere inside me, a dam is holding

back a Niagara Falls of tears. I'm in mourning, but I haven't been able to let it out yet.

I miss my grandchildren. I'm so afraid they'll be strangers when this is all over, if it's ever over. I miss Amanda; I miss talking to Kendall and Anthony. I miss calling to cheer up my precious parents, and my long hours at the computer. I miss my pumpkin shell, for there Rick kept me very well.

But the pumpkin shell is no more. A mosquito blew it to bits.

Wednesday, September 12

I wonder when — if — his preaching voice will ever return. That confident authority, the sure words, the unquestionable intelligence. He knows so much about everything. For thirty-one years I've lived with a walking, talking reference book. I used it, too, and often told him often how I admired his mind, especially since mine is so often vacant.

Tonight I read the first few chapters of the book of Job aloud.

"Hon, why does Job's first counsellor get so much criticism?" I asked. "What's wrong with his advice to Job?"

He kept his eyes shut and shook his head. "Never thought about it," he barely whispered.

He has. I know he has. But those thoughts have been locked behind the door of pain and weariness, and only God has the key.

⌐

This morning Amanda called.

I could hear the children in the background. It sounded like a pre-school. Kendall had a ministerial meeting, she said. (Kendall pastors Ebenezer Baptist Church, fifteen minutes north of Yorkton.) Was there a chance that Grandma Gerry could stay with Dad while I came home for lunch with her and the Beans? They missed me, she said.

I could hear the biggest Bean in the background chanting, "Nana ... Nana, Nana."

"He's having his own conversation with you on our old cell phone," Amanda said.

I offered to talk to him, but he wouldn't talk to the real me. Only to the imaginary me at the other end of the cell phone. And they were having jolly good conversation.

Perhaps he *was* talking to the real me, the one who lived a real life and did things with him. Baked cookies and went for walks to construction sites, slid down red and yellow slides, mucked about in bare feet in mud puddles.

That me is so far gone from me that I fear I may never find her again.

But I did go home for lunch. For two hours I trusted that God and Mom would take care of the other half of my heart. And I played with Amanda and the children, ate with the children, changed their diapers, and rejoiced in their tiny, perfect bodies.

And Tabatha walked for me. Four straight steps, into my arms, holding her own out at her side to balance her bobbling body. In the circle of my embrace, she said, "Mmm, mmm, mmmm ..." She does that with every hug.

"You're walking, Tabatha girl," I squealed.

I looked up. Behind her came Benjamin.

"My walking!" he sang, his tone a precise replica of my own, holding his hands at his side and weaving just like Tabatha did — right into the circle of my arms, where Tabatha was already cuddled up under my chin.

And so we hugged, the three of us. And I wondered if the day would come when someone else, someone very large, would walk into our circle, too.

Saturday, September 15
E-mail Update

Friends, Family, Readers (and Strangers!),

Several have requested a more recent update on Rick to read in their churches on Sunday. We have cause for joy.

An ENT (ear, nose, and throat) specialist examined him this week. We made an agonizing journey, on wheels, one that entailed numerous upchucking stops, into the bowels of the hospital. Our journey ended at a wee hobbit hole where this out-of-town specialist sets up practice for two or three days every few weeks.

The good doctor gave Rick a thorough inspection and proclaimed, almost in surprise, "There's no paralysis of this man's vocal cords, which is something we frequently see in severe cases of West Nile."

We're so grateful that despite all their plundering, the pirates of the West Nile left this treasure undisturbed. And his ears have been touched only slightly, another cause for joy.

Thanks once more for your prayers, kind calls, and so much more. You've all been so kind and dear — our family truly couldn't do this without you.

Still trusting,
Kathleen

P.S. For those of a more theological bent: We're reading the book of Job most nights beside his hospital bed, Rick and I. The book indisputably demonstrates that God sometimes allows illness as a test of our faith.

But some faith teachers, whose students may be among the readers of my updates (since these updates have found wings of their own far beyond my knowledge), insist it's never God's will for us to be ill. They cleverly twist scripture to bypass the necessity of pain — even God-allowed pain — for growth.

Such teaching, to both Rick and me, results in a horrific aborting of God's sufficient grace and belittles a God that scripture clearly represents as big enough to carry us through even the deepest, darkest valleys, kicking and screaming, perhaps, but through nevertheless. He's even big enough to sustain us in permanent conditions. Consider those with the kind of sicknesses no popular faith healer will even allow on their platforms.

In almost half a century as a Christ-follower, I've learned and observed that God, whether we like it or not, allows trouble to come to his children, even his best-behaved ones (consider Christ!), and does so for good reasons. Discipline, perhaps. A demonstration of his glory. Even for the purpose of death. Read what David said, in Psalm 119:71-77, about his own troubles:

> *It was good for me to be afflicted so that I might learn your decrees.*
> *The law from your mouth is more precious to me than thousands of pieces of silver and gold.*
> *Your hands made me and formed me; give me understanding to learn your commands.*
> *May those who fear you rejoice when they see me, for I have put my hope in your word.*
> *I know, O LORD, that your laws are righteous, and in faithfulness you have afflicted me.*
> *May your unfailing love be my comfort, according to your promise to your servant.*
> *Let your compassion come to me that I may live, for your law is my delight.*

Jesus also said that only the weak demand a sign (a miracle?), and James calls on us to persevere through trials so we may be made full and complete.

God has, over the years, accompanied Rick and me through shadowed valleys of many kinds — some of our own making. So far we've exited alive, and when the day comes that we don't, we expect it will only be because there's a better place for us than this troubled old world, a place where we will be fully alive.

Why do we choose not to kick and scream and thrash about, looking for a quick exit from the pirates' attack?

Because we've come to trust God implicitly to lead and guide us to an ending yet unseen. We'd rather be carried in his arms through the mess the pirates left behind than be ejected painlessly on the safe shore and have missed the sweet communion with him the Bible calls "the fellowship of his sufferings."

Rick and I discussed this yesterday, and even through veils of pain, he whispered, "I want to learn what God wants me to in this."

It's times like this we have both preached about, written about, and testified about all our adult lives. If we were to insist that he provide us a quick exit, how small and meaningless our faith would be. We are in constant contact with the God who created Rick the first time, and can, if he *wishes*, create him all over again. He knows what we need, Jesus tells us in Matthew 6, so we are to make our request and not go on babbling like the pagans.

Honestly, sometimes we do babble, I confess — especially when the pain gets too much.

— Kathleen

Adapted from my online birding column, *September 7*

A few months ago, a friend and I drove the highway that runs parallel with and only a few hundred yards beyond the Pacific coastline. She spotted something and pulled over.

"Look," she said, pointing. Excitement raised her voice above its usual melodic contralto.

Just beyond the reach of the tide's edge, four or five bald eagles, some mature, some still waiting for their white caps, cavorted on a large driftwood snag.

We watched until the last eagle flew off, screeching, "Wait up," or so it seemed, to the rest who had gone on ahead.

The Bible repeatedly refers to God's wings, as well as to the eagle's strength and majesty and its soaring flight. People of strong faith, says our holy book, will do the same.

Those words have created in Rick a fascination for eagles. Parishioners and friends know this, and if they don't, all they have to do is walk into his office.

Inside the door, with a little imagination, one can feel an updraft from mighty wings. Lining the top shelf of his wrap-around computer desk, hanging on the walls, perched on shelves, are dozens of eagles — ceramic, wood, brass, glass sculptures — in every imaginable position.

The only birds Rick sees these days are the pigeons that regularly perform fly-pasts on the other side of his hospital room window. The pirates of West Nile saw to that. Our hoped-for long days of sunlit side-by-side flights are in jeopardy.

Nevertheless, I've never appreciated eagles as much as I do these days. The sculptures I appreciate most are still the ones of eagles with wings outstretched, the ones soaring on unseen currents, their binocular eyes on the ground below as they wait for a motion, a movement, a hint of anything that suggests a good thing may be just around the corner.

Our wings are outstretched, our eyes ready.

Monday, September 17

I opened my eyes to another golden September morning. The kind I think about when I hear the words of the song, "Deep in December ... it's nice to remember ... September ..." A day blue and gold, autumn dressed for a ball. A dancing day, full of promise. But I struggled for motivation to rise.

Rick and I have prayed the same prayer for twenty-seven days, ever since the pirates first attacked. "Lord, give us strength for the day, and bright hope for tomorrow." He's answered that prayer every single day. "Do it again today, please, God," I plead.

~

A stranger stopped me as I rushed across the hospital parking lot.

"Excuse me, ma'am," he said. "Where'd you get that?" He pointed to the rolled-up sheepskin I carried.

I was already later than usual, and in a hurry. A neighbour had phoned and I had talked too long. Then, rushing out to the car, I realized I had forgotten the sheepskin. I had promised to bring it for Rick, thinking it would help ease his pain if I placed it under him. I rushed back into the house to find it.

"I raise horses," the stranger continued. "I need something like that to wrap around their legs."

"Sorry, I honestly can't remember where I bought it," I said. "We've had it for years."

I eased away, but he seemed eager to talk. A baby boy had joined his family the night before, he told me. I congratulated him, explaining that my husband was recovering from West Nile disease.

"West Nile? Really!" he said, his face sobering.

Our conversation over, the young man wished us all the best.

"What room's your husband in?" he asked, curiously.

I told him, then hurried away.

Less than half an hour later, he walked into that hospital room with a vase of burgundy carnations in one hand and a photo in the other. Setting the flowers on the table, he leaned over the Preacher, shoved the photo in his face, and said firmly, "Sir, you don't know me, I don't know you, but I want you to look at this picture."

His surprise announcement drew the Preacher from his veil of pain. His eyes flew open to see a photo of two beribboned champion draft horses.

"These are my horses, and they're West Nile survivors," the man said. "If they could beat it, you can, too. You gotta pray, trust God, and believe."

He prayed for the Preacher then, a simple prayer that must have gone straight to the heart of God. A prayer for strength and hope, for healing and faith.

All I knew was this: In his perfect timing, God orchestrated our meeting in that hospital parking lot. God had answered my morning prayer for hope.

A few hours later a nurse entered the room. "We're moving you again tomorrow," she said with a smile. "By ambulance. A bed has become available at the rehab centre."

Monday, September 17
E-mail Update

Family and Friends,

Today we got the news: A bed has opened up for Rick in Wascana Rehabilitation Centre. I'm so grateful — and a little intimidated, honestly. Wascana is in Regina, two hours away. Because the facility encourages family to be part of the rehab care, I've decided to stay in Regina for the duration of his time there.

This move means a sharp increase in what will be expected of Rick, so please pray, mostly for his healing and determination to push on with God's help. Also pray that God will continue to provide exactly what we need: strength for each day, hope for each tomorrow, teachable spirits, clear heads, courage, and patience.

Thanks so much,
Kathleen and Rick

Tuesday, September 18

Mom and I walked into the room early this morning to help Rick prepare for his transfer. Behind the curtain, we could hear his voice groaning, pleading: "Hurry, please, please, please, hurry."

Mom poked me. "Go in," she said, panic raising her usually calm voice.

I peered around the curtain. Two nurses were transferring Rick off the commode back into bed. But he was slumped in the harness of the sit-to-stand lift, hanging by his armpits, his knees limp and splayed out of the black knee grooves, crying like a baby. Later he said the moment reminded him of the classic poster of the cat hanging by one claw at the end of a rope.

"Stand up, Rick," the nurse encouraged. "You have one good leg!"

I walked up behind her. "Actually, he has no good legs," I said.

I could hear ice and fury in my own voice, both struggling for release.

Startled, she turned and proceeded to lower him.

Back on the bed, Rick sobbed, his shoulders heaving. In thirty-one years, I've never seen him more broken. I put my arms around him. Wishing just to take him home. To abort this story here and now.

"It's all right, hon. I'm here now."

"Rick, Rick," one of the nurses said, in dismay.

I must remember this: They don't understand his weakness, this disease, its physical or emotional fallout.

And this: We must not be silent.

I thanked the doctor before we left. I also said, "I'm sure you're glad to be getting rid of this troublesome wife, but I've only got one husband and I won't stop fighting for him, no matter what."

He seemed surprised, but wished us well.

⌒

Kendall drove me to Regina in his van. If I need it, I'll arrange to have the car brought later. Mom Gibson sat up front. I chose to sit in the back seat with Benjamin, pretending I was a real grandmother without a care in the world. One who sings silly songs and makes silly faces and reads silly books about alphabet letters climbing up to the top of a coconut tree and tumbling back again. Chick-a-chick-a-boom-boom.

At Wascana, a nurse ushered Rick's gurney into a lovely semi-private room.

"Not much of a view," Mom said, looking out a flat gravelled roof just outside the window and the brick wall opposite. But I could see sky. For me, any window that allows a peek at the sky is a room with a view.

Mom stayed with Rick while I took Benjamin to my new digs in the hostel at the other end of the hospital. For as long as I am able, as long as God provides, I'll rent this ten foot by twelve foot cement room, three stories up, its window filled from corner to corner with a large maple, the sky visible from between its leaves. I not only have a view, but an exquisite one.

I also have my own toilet and shower, a very comfortable single bed, a chair, a desk, and a closet. I am able-bodied, and I live in luxury.

I returned to Rick's room alone after the rest had headed back to Yorkton.

This place is a massive brick complex, with over three hundred beds. So far, all I've seen is maze of hallways, elevated walkways, and vaulted glass ceilings. I've also noticed some unusual visitors: dogs — large, small, medium — led by their owners along these halls. Pets, I've heard, are welcome visitors. This is our brave new world.

Wednesday, September 19

Once a week, for as long as Rick remains here, he will have "clinic," when all those regularly connected to his care will meet to assess his progress. Sometimes we'll be invited to join.

This happened today. But rather than make him come to the conference room — handily right across the hall — his care team trooped into his room and stood around his bed.

We met Rick's new doctor, Dr. Todd Yip, who specializes in physiatry (a specialization I hadn't heard of, involving the way the body moves); his two primary therapists: Maggie, from occupational therapy (upper body) and Errin, from physiotherapy (lower body); the charge nurse (Linda, today); the floor supervisor, Sharon; and Tracie, the social worker (every patient is assigned one, I'm told).

Including Rick in every part of the discussion, each person contributed questions and thoughts on how best to help, what they felt about what had been done so far, what their role on Rick's team would be, what they felt should be changed from the Yorkton plan.

The blessing of being included as an important part of my husband's care almost overwhelmed me. I'm part of a team, hallelujah!

Rick worked so hard in his first therapy sessions today that his body revolted. His pain was tremendous, and after supper his nausea began again, wave after wave. He retched several times, and worried about calling the nurses.

"Don't worry, hon," I said. "This will all work itself out."

"Even the birds don't go through this," he said. "They just die."

"You're not getting off that easy."

Thursday, September 20

When I walked into Rick's room at 7:30 this morning, Maggie, Rick's lovely occupational therapist, was already working with him on practical skills, beginning with teaching him adaptive methods to feed and dress himself. She had brought cutlery designed for people with hand limitations, a hook for reaching things, a sock tube, and numerous smaller things that may prove invaluable in the days ahead.

As I pushed Rick's wheelchair to PT (physical therapy), Rick complained that taking the elevator upset his stomach.

"Okay, next time we take the stairs," I told him.

I forgot. I honestly forgot. Our new normal includes a wheelchair.

It happened later, too. When we left OT (occupational therapy), the double entry door was open only on one side. I left Rick's chair to open the other one.

As I reached for the latch at the top, I heard Rick say, "See ya."

In our real life, that would have meant he'd found an easier way out and was heading there himself. I turned around to follow. There he sat, like a gray wizard, his chair rolling gently backwards — and he couldn't do a thing to stop it.

I have a few things to learn about caring for someone with a disability, I think. Rick agrees.

His new doctor has ordered the removal of his catheter, but Rick's bladder refuses to go back to work. So do his bowels. The staff are retraining his bladder with tubes, measuring its contents with portable ultrasound, as well as every drop that emerges. They have also instituted "bowel care" nights, using a veritable arsenal of tools: enemas, laxatives, stool softeners — not to mention rubber gloves.

Nothing about this is comfortable for Rick, but all the attention has its good side: quality time with the staff, who are getting to know him as a person, not merely a patient.

We laughed this evening — yes, Rick laughed. Lots. As one of the nurses worked over him tonight, we began telling stories about people we worked with during our college days, as part-time aides in a nursing home. The nurses giggled at his laughter.

Here, they transfer Rick with a "people crane," as I call the power lift. They have ruled out the sit-to-stand lift; house rules dictate that a patient must be able to stand for several seconds unassisted to use that lift. Such a rule at the hospital back home may have saved his shoulder, which is still out of joint and excruciatingly painful.

Maggie measured Rick for a correctly sized wheelchair today. The one he's been using is a lovely black vehicle, but very large, even for him. While measuring, she mentioned that the chair can go home with him when he is discharged. My brain refuses to accept what my ears heard.

Friday, September 21
E-mail Update

Family and Friends,

We are moved now, both of us temporary residents within the healing halls of Wascana Rehabilitation Centre. We thank God hourly for the provision of these beds: Rick's, on a rehab ward, mine in a rented room in the hospital hostel.

The staff here have been exceptional. They understand the need, in treating Rick's condition, to strike a balance between aggressive focused therapy and quiet rest, the latter mandatory for the brain to recover from the assault of the pirates.

Another name has been added to that list of pirates that have assaulted our little boat: Poliomyelitis joins West Nile disease, encephalitis, and meningoencephalitis. The names swirl in the befuddling brine surrounding us in this sea of sickness. Sometimes they threaten to overwhelm us. Thankfully, long ago we asked Jesus to board our craft, and despite the threats, we're holding steady.

Nighttimes are the worst hours for Rick. They were in Yorkton, too. The pain and the nausea descend then, in waves, as though punishing him for daring to impose activity on his lazy limbs during the day. And time moves twice as slowly in the dark, he says.

Regardless of the number of times Rick has had to call in the night, no one on the staff we've met in these first few days has made us feel that we're imposing.

To one of the staff, he voiced a concern that if he called too often they might string him up.

"We don't string our patients up on their first nights," one of the nurses said. "Now, if you try it a second night ..."

He did — does. They haven't come through on their threat yet.

Rick is currently having three forty-five minute therapy sessions a day, building on the good work begun by Melissa in Yorkton.

"What are your goals for your time here at Wascana?" Errin, his physiotherapist, asked him, during his first session.

He thought awhile.

"My left arm is weak," he said slowly, then paused, as though waiting for inspiration.

"Uh huh? ..." Errin said.

"I need it to drive my scooter," he said finally.

I could see her suppress a smile as she asked about his scooter. Then she said, "I can tell your scooter is really important to you. But perhaps there are a few other goals we should work on first. Like getting you able to sit up on your own."

The positive atmosphere in the therapy rooms is palpable, despite some of the desperate conditions we've observed. That might have something to do with the sign hanging in the physiotherapy room: "Faith, Hope, and Therapy," it reads.

Our journey down the West Nile has shown us our intense need for all three of those.

Faith to believe that, as the Word says, God is even now working all this to our good.

Hope that tomorrow the pain will be less, the nurses will remain understanding, and God will use this for his glory.

And therapy, which God can use to bring healing and health once more to Rick's limbs.

The Psalms are a daily inspiration and the best kind of counsellor. On the 20th, it was Psalm 20. Try reading that one next time you're sick in bed. You'll find it exactly what Doctor God ordered.

I asked Rick tonight if he wanted to say something special to all our family and friends. He had one word: "pray."

Thank you so much for your continued prayers for both of us.

Blessings and love,
Kathleen and Rick

SUNNY SIDE UP
September 26

Champions Persist Despite Obstacles

The Preacher and I watched an astonishing reality show last summer. The show's star, Valiant, had the formidable task of transporting, without vehicle or beast, a monumental cargo across a vast tract of wilderness. Every moment of the journey was fraught with peril.

Attacked by vicious crosswinds, nearly annihilated by mammoth-sized creatures, ignored by observers (who could have helped, but didn't), and observed by giants (who could have eliminated the smaller traveller, and also didn't), Valiant soldiered on.

The truth? The Preacher and I were the giants, and Moses, our cat, was the mammoth-sized creature. Our back patio was the wilderness, and Valiant was a tiny red ant hauling home his prize — a dead dragonfly — one millimeter at a time.

Larger ants scurried by, tracing a wide path around the little guy with the big load. Not once did the wee being stop trying. Pushing, pulling, crawling sideways, forward, backward, Valiant worked harder than any creature I've ever seen, battling both the weight of the dragonfly and a wind that felt brisk even to us giants.

At one point a particularly strong gust tucked itself under the larger insect's wing and the pair became airborne.

They landed intact, Valiant still clinging to his prize. He dragged it backwards, into the cat's tail fur just as the tail twitched. Both insects flew into orbit.

The ant landed, separated from its prize by several inches.

"Scurry home, Valiant," I said. "Surely this old thing isn't worth risking your life."

But the insect immediately returned to the dragonfly, grabbed it again, and resumed its arduous journey, scuttling sideways this time, two steps forward, three back.

He finally made it across the twenty or so feet of cement, hauled the dragonfly into the grass jungle where the wind couldn't interfere, and disappeared. Homeward bound, we assumed. Several anthills border the patio there.

"Yea," I hooted. "He made it! What a champion! A valiANT, persistANT, ChampiANT."

We don't love ants, the Preacher and I. They're impolite at picnics. They make our skin crawl. Sometimes they bite. But after watching Valiant's struggle, we certainly have greater respect for them.

Consider this: To match the feat of that quarter-inch ant, we humans would have to walk over a thousand miles carrying a load of at least five hundred pounds — and do it all in fifteen minutes.

Take a lesson from Valiant: Persist, no matter what the opposition. God enables his children to carry our loads in ways we'll never comprehend.

Saturday, September 22

With the exception of a sweet-sounding mandolin orchestra that practices in the vast concourse every Saturday morning, weekends are quiet here. There are no scheduled therapy sessions and the office staff doesn't work. The ward halls are quieter, too. Some of the patients go home.

We had company today. Our good friends, Ken and Sharon Dressler, brought Mom Gibson to be with us for her final few days in Saskatchewan before her flight back east.

I dressed Rick in a new shirt, a soft, brown knit, long-sleeved one with a few buttons at the front. Sitting up in the wheelchair, he looked almost himself, except for the shoulder harness Maggie has fashioned to try to keep his shoulder bones together. His eyes have become huge in his newly gaunt face.

Rather than visit in his wardroom, I wheeled Rick, at school zone speed, down to the small atrium at the far end of the concourse. The rest followed in a royal procession. Rick didn't participate much in the discussion, but we sat there talking for at least half an hour, until he became nauseous and fatigued.

As we made our way back, we met two pleasant-looking young women, both in black wheelchairs. The second snuggled just behind and followed close to the first, so that the pair of chairs resembled two cogs in a wheel.

Wheelchairs are a common mode of transport on the concourse. But this sighting startled us because as the chairs neared us we noticed something unique. The first girl, by her clever arrangement of the chairs, was propelling not only herself but her friend as well.

Even more startling were the smiles that were stretching broadly across their faces.

I've been using the sea-blue prayer shawl from St. Paul's Lutheran Church ever since Jolene gave it to us that first day in ICU. I used it in the hospital rooms back home, to throw over my shoulders when the air felt chilly, but it covers me at night now, and reminds me of the song, "Cover me, Lord, with your presence ..." When I throw it over my shoulders, I can feel our friends' prayers warming me.

The idea of a prayer covering is a biblical one, and one I find particularly helpful in this often chilly place. Rick has a prayer shawl now, too, soft and gray as a barn kitten. Our friend Rita Rodney knit it, and I throw it over his shoulders often. He asks for it when I forget.

⌒

May Leong, our precious friend who lives here in Regina, picked me up tonight. I left Rick in Mom's care and on this golden September day walked with May around Wascana Lake, across the street from the rehab centre. The sight of whole-bodied people biking, skateboarding, jogging brought me a keen sense of pleasure and wonder at the gift of movement — and fresh awareness of its precarious fragility.

Following our walk, we picked up veggie submarine sandwiches and ate them beside the lake, which was polka-dotted with geese, seagulls, and ducks bedding down for the night. A flock of greedy seagulls loitered near our bench. I tossed them a few bits of my sandwich. Several dove for it immediately, shoving each other aside.

"Don't do that!" May said.

"Why not?"

"Because you make them fight and you only have enough for one, and they are going to bed and you make them wake up for a nighttime snack and then you give them false hope!"

Her words came out in such a comical rush, I couldn't stop laughing.

At dusk, beneath a pinking sky, I exited the real world through the front doors of the Wascana, back into my West Nile exile.

⌒

Rick didn't settle well tonight. I had to turn him numerous times to keep him comfortable. His bowels still haven't moved, despite numerous tiny cups of medicine. His automatic downspout still isn't functioning on its own, either. I prayed with him, said goodnight, and left his room for the last time at 10:30.

Sunday September 23

It's 3:40 p.m. as I write this. I'm sitting beside Rick's bed. On our tape player, Kate Smith sings, "... I'm alone with my memories of you."

Memories. Something I've tried hard to not dwell on, especially during that walk last night with May. How often Rick and I have walked around that lake, sometimes hand in hand, enjoying the scenery. This is the (mostly) comfortable companionship of the long married, though I remember at least once chafing the entire way because I wanted to walk and talk, and he only to walk and walk.

We didn't walk together half enough.

These days, these desperate days, have driven us closer than we were ever able to become back in our real life, even when we were both full-bodied, like the cups of tea we enjoyed most afternoons in our parsonage living room. But on too many days, those few minutes were the closest we came to each other.

When we get to the other side of this tunnel, we won't be the same pair we were. The pirates have seen to that already. In this sense perhaps they've done us a great favour.

⌒

Today's score from the ongoing battle of the bowels: one for the Preacher, zero for the pirates.

Mom and I sat in her hostel room and chatted this evening like college girls.

"I'm glad my son is married to you," she said as we said goodnight.

Monday, September 24

Rick is fighting nausea again today.

I woke early, but went back to sleep and didn't drag myself out of bed until quarter to seven. When I walked into Rick's room, I found Mom quietly watching Maggie work with him, teaching him some of the very things she had taught him to do a half-century ago. How to wash up. How to put deodorant on (a particular challenge with one arm). I watched her, watching them, and thought how strange it all must feel.

After Maggie left, the breakfast tray arrived. Guests, too: Larry and Audrey Dahl. Rick seemed quite animated while they were with us, and I'm sure they'll pass on a good report on how well he's doing.

The report won't include the price of the good show Rick put on, because they won't know about it.

Nearly every time Rick puts out the extra effort to visit, he pays for it later. It's almost as though his brain taxes his whole body for the good performance, however short.

Strangely, he doesn't remember most of the visitors who stopped by in Yorkton — or much else from that first month. I remind him by reading him excerpts from my journal.

I never again want to take for granted the blessing of natural, healthy movement. Most well people can simply sit up by themselves and walk away. These days we're learning the mechanics of disability, especially the business of transporting a very ill, mostly paralyzed person. I took notes today as we prepared Rick for his trip downstairs to physio:

With Rick still in bed, lower the bed head and allow him to use the bottle as a preventative strike against "the urge" arriving during physio; wait for the staff to come and measure what flowed into the bottle, record that number on his input/output sheet, wait for them to go get his Gravol and Tylenol to brace him for the pain and nausea physio causes, get a glass of water and a straw with which to down the pills, raise the bed head, give him the pills and water, mark the amount of fluid he took to down the pills on the input/output sheet, wait for the staff to go find the lift, wait again while they look for the correct lift-tag colour (black), put the bed down into a lying position, help Rick roll onto his right side by lifting his left arm up and out of the way and then over to the right-hand-side bedrail so he can grab it and assist with the roll. Stick the harness under him, with half of it rolled up lengthwise, help him roll onto the other side, connect the lift straps, put the wheelchair into place, allow the lift to pick him up off the bed like a bag of relief goods and swing him in the direction of the wheelchair, then gently lower him. Raise him again because he's not quite far enough back, and have someone push the wheel-chair into better position. Once in the chair, undo the straps connecting him to the harness. Now tug at the back and at each hip to remove the harness. Look for the shoulder holster Maggie designed to try to keep his shoulder in place. Cuff and strap it around his left arm, fastening the three Velcro straps, winding the long strap across his back, under his right arm and back across his back. Loop it through the metal ring, tug it tightly, and fasten the end to the other side of the Velcro strap. Now put on his sandals, lift his feet up onto the footrests, fasten his seatbelt, send someone to get the chart from the desk, take off the brakes, make for the door, stop, run back into the room to grab the kidney basin and a towel (just in case) and proceed to the elevator. Wait three turns for the elevator to empty. Push Rick's chair into elevator, turn it around in elevator, get off on the right floor, proceed out and down the long hall to physio — all at school zone speed. Arrive at physio.

Easy.

Tuesday, September 25

On this golden September day — far too nice to be indoors — I turned fifty-one.

I count myself blessed. I can't think of anyone I'd rather spend my birthday with than Rick, and I got to spend the entire day with him.

Benjamin Bean called: "Happy Day Day, Nana. You, You!" He kept repeating it, louder and louder. I think he was singing. He ended with, "I u oo!"

Mom G. is worried that I'm not taking care of myself. We sat in her room tonight for one last visit before she leaves tomorrow. How I love this little woman. She deserves so much more than I was able to give her on this trip.

Wednesday, September 26

Life moves slowly here, as it should, considering that healing seldom happens quickly, and to cooperate with the body's processes, we must slow down, even be still.

But the stillness is kind of ache in itself. The slow movement of the wheelchair. The time it takes for every blessed thing. The waiting for the hours to pass for the next pill, and then the waiting for it to take effect.

In today's morning therapy, Rick shared a couch with a little girl. A dark-skinned child whose father doesn't speak English. She was all smiles and twinkle, though horribly handicapped. She beamed at me from her flat-backed position on the bed as the therapist manipulated her legs.

Clinic today. We rolled across the hall into the circle of friends sitting there — all with the purpose of rebuilding our little boat. Rebuilding Rick. The discussion swirled around goals, accomplishments, the effectiveness of meds, the bowel problem.

Rick contributed well, articulating slowly but clearly his feelings about the process we have begun.

"How are you doing with your goal of walking?" Errin asked.

"Well ..." He paused to think. "I'm not there yet."

Everyone had the grace not to smirk.

Tonight it seemed the pirates won a skirmish. Our four-hour struggle with that inflamed nerve in his left leg left us both utterly exhausted. No pain medication could touch it, and I wondered if the pain would literally drive Rick past distraction. It was his most arduous hour since arriving here.

I moved his legs, shifted his body, rubbed on liniment, prayed, read scripture, read Bill Cosby — sweet comedic relief — sang, held him as he cried, covered him, uncovered him, smoothed out the ridges under him from his restless shifting, and felt utterly helpless.

No pain medication helps with the worst of this pain. Finally, around midnight, the nurses came with a new sleeping pill, ordered by Dr. Yip just today. Fifteen minutes later, Rick lay sleeping like a baby, naked except for his paper brief and a flannelette blanket.

And I crept home to my little room.

Thursday, September 27

He didn't talk much today, even in his therapy sessions. The pain, or perhaps the encephalitis, took him away from me again. Into his safe box where he retreats when he can't handle noise and conversation.

After PT this morning, I asked him if he wanted me to wheel him into the patient lounge at the end of the hall. I could see Don and Glenda Bell down there. Don has West Nile, too.

"Okay, but I don't want to talk," he said.

"Are you thinking about something when you go quiet like that?" I asked him later.

"Yes," he said, surprising me. Usually he says, "No."

"What?"

"How I can get rid of this pain."

"Do you still believe?"

"Believe what?"

"Everything. All you've ever preached about trouble, and loss, and God being there in our times of trial."

He nodded.

"You're not tempted to curse God and die, like Job?"

He shook his head.

Friday, September 28
E-mail Update

Hello, Friends, Family, and Readers,

To those who have been consistent and faithful in prayer — thank you. These reports are especially for you. God is answering your prayers. Like any journey, some days are up, some down. I'll say first that God is still supplying strength for the day — some days not much extra, but "sufficient" (which is all he promised).

Rick still spends most of his time in bed, and much of that in pain. He needs less help now to roll from side to side, and we're down to three pillows from seven — that's progress.

If you've ever known anyone who's had a bad stroke, the recovery is similar. Movements once effortless have become formidable challenges.

Yesterday Maggie, Rick's occupational therapist, spent considerable time making him work the fingers of his left arm: digging them into a stiff pink therapy "dough" and dragging them across it.

Errin, his physiotherapist, works each day on his legs. Much of that is done while he is lying flat on a mat. She works hard at making him move, resist, and rock.

But yesterday they rolled his wheelchair (oh yes, he has his own wheelchair now — a temporary vehicle, we anticipate) over to something called a standing frame, a machine that lifts him (well and safely harnessed) and holds him in a standing position so his back and leg muscles can strengthen and remember their jobs. He stood for three minutes yesterday. Errin was impressed.

The encephalitis part of the pirates' attack may well take the longest to rehabilitate. He finds noise, commotion, or change extremely unsettling. Too many voices at once make him withdraw and sometimes he hides in a place that I can't reach at all. He always comes back eventually, and we're both learning to be patient with the process. On a really good day, he jokes and laughs with the staff, a great bunch of people we're coming to love.

Rick has lost forty pounds since entering hospital — not a diet plan either one of us would recommend.

What amazes me about the shadowed valleys we have traversed is how light cohabits with dark. We tend to think of these two extremes as mutually exclusive. They're not. Through our years as Christ-followers, when we've looked for it, we've found light that would have been nigh invisible in untroubled times: always God, guiding, comforting, bringing hope through the strangest and most unlikely of means. I've observed this again and again in the last forty days.

From fresh experience with the fragility of life, allow me to offer you some hard-won advice:

Please come home early sometimes, just to enjoy each other, to be still together, to enjoy your homes or to walk hand in hand or do together whatever helps you shut out the rest of the world for a while.

Forget about work and debt and kids and problems, and focus on being grateful for the wondrous gifts God has given. His Son. Life. Love. Movement. We are truly "as grass," as the Bible says, and may not have the opportunity tomorrow.

Faith,
Kathleen and Rick

Saturday, September 29

The Beans visited today. While we waited for them, I wheeled Rick down to the concourse, thinking we'd sit in the sun and enjoy a spell of visiting and people-watching.

Rick had a different idea.

I pulled his wheelchair next to a set of children's paintings decorating one of the concourse walls.

"Don't stop," he barked.

We've been working on those "pleases," but sometimes he forgets to use them on me. I wheeled his chair around and began the long walk down to the end of the concourse.

On one of the walls there's a mural of a lake, like the one we left before the pirates attacked.

"Look, hon," I said. "Isn't this well done?"

"Keep moving," he barked.

"Well, I don't see how moving helps," I said, allowing myself a slight complaint. It's not my nature to serve uncomplainingly.

"I don't know either, but it does," he said.

So we moved. And kept moving. Until even moving didn't relieve his pain, so I rolled him back upstairs, where the nurses used the lift to hoist him back into bed.

When the children arrived, Tabatha's adorable face, peering up from her stroller, rounded the corner first. The rest followed, flowing into our room like blessed breezes after too much heat.

But Rick had worried about their visit. That he wouldn't be well enough to visit well. That they may be too much for him. I think he worried himself sick, actually. He didn't enjoy the day.

When we left Rick's room tonight, we headed for my hostel room. While Amanda and Kendall were getting Tabatha in her jammies for the ride home, Benjamin followed me into the washroom.

"I need to wash," he said.

I held him up to the sink, where he used a facecloth to wash his hands and arms and face. As I began to lower him, he said, "And tongue, Nana!"

"Oh," I said, "yes, we can't forget the tongue."

Not until he had scrubbed his tongue thoroughly with the facecloth was he ready to leave Nana's bathroom.

Tabatha walks everywhere now, standing as tall as a one-year-old can. She turns too suddenly sometimes and falls over, crawls for a while, then gets up on her own.

"Nana," she said to me at lunchtime, and repeated it: "Nana, Nana, Nana, Nana."

I had told Benjamin we would go see the lake and the birds before they left town. Time slipped away on us. How I hate making a promise to a child and breaking it, especially to my Beans. Instead, I showed him lake pictures on my camera. I also played him a little video I took the other day of the nurses transferring Rick from the bed to the chair. He sat spellbound, watching the process.

They left in the rain. I ran out and poked my head into the van to say goodbye.

"Nana, come in van," Benjamin said. "Nana, come Nana's *house!*"

Sunday, September 30

Today we pretended we were real people, with real lives, like the one we had before the West Nile pirates attacked our little boat. Because the staff knew we wanted to go to the facility's Protestant church service at 1:30, they didn't get Rick up until almost lunch-time, which consisted of half an egg salad sandwich, a small tossed salad, and a banana.

I pushed Rick's chair down to the second-floor chapel — past the cafeteria, round a left corner, down a long ramp, and through the labyrinth of halls that lead into the old part of this building, the portion that houses the long-term residents. Most are no longer candidates for rehabilitation. Most, it seems, exist only to those who care for them here.

I don't know what I expected. I don't know what Rick expected. The chapel itself seemed in character: a spacious room with a slightly raised platform and an electric piano. Flat blue carpet on the floor, quilted hangings with a creation theme on the wall. Exceptional stained-glass windows, oak furniture, and an overhead screen.

But somehow I didn't expect a nursing-home service of the kind Rick has led himself countless times, in a room full of elderly people whiffling and calling and shifting, sneezing, snorting, and complaining.

I counted nineteen people in wheelchairs, thirteen in regular chairs. I parked Rick near the door in front of a nice-looking gentleman in a wheelchair.

The nice-looking gentleman roared like a lion through the entire service. When he wasn't roaring, in a voice that sounded as though it was coming from beneath a rocky river bottom, he called, "Food. I need food. Give me food."

I looked over at Rick once during that, and caught his lips twitching.

The roars continued, despite another patient's "Oh, shut up. Keep your mouth closed."

I snuck a glance at the man in the wheelchair next to me. Sitting upright, brow furrowed, gray beard resting on his upper chest, staring straight ahead, expressionless.

Oh, Rick, my love, I thought. We didn't mean to get here so soon, did we?

I don't remember much else about the service. An older woman, full of strength and vitality, preached. An even older man, the lady preacher's mate, I think, played the piano as vigorously as she preached. Their daughter led the singing.

As we left, Rick stuck out his hand to the woman preacher.

"God bless you," he said fervently.

Following the church service, a girls' choir, dressed nattily in burgundy school sweaters, gave a concert in the concourse. Their voices, young and pure, soared like our Amanda's did when she was a teenager. "Sometimes I Feel Like a Motherless Child," sang an amazing young black girl with stiff orange tips on the end of her hair. Me, too, I thought.

We arrived back at Rick's room, three and a half hours after we had left. He was utterly spent. But the afternoon was another landmark on the journey: He had spent four solid hours in his chair.

Monday, October 1

Most of today Rick sat staring straight ahead.

On his darkest days he complains about feeling "different," like he's "behind a wall" and can't get around it. The nurses feel he should have antidepressants, and he's ready to agree.

"Does it irritate you, when I'm cheerful and you're feeling so down?" I asked.

"Only sometimes."

SUNNY SIDE UP
October 3, 2007

Grateful for What Remains

The other day, while the Preacher slept, I slipped from his bedside to wander the spacious concourse of his temporary home at Regina's Wascana Rehabilitation Centre. Ceilings soared several stories above me, glossy floors stretched far ahead of me. To my left, vast windows let in the magnificent autumn light.

I strolled past tall indoor trees and numerous arrangements of comfortable couches and sat down to chat with new friends. The pirates attacked their little boat, too.

While we visited, I observed the passers-by: people in all stages of health — some in, or pushing wheelchairs, others strolling or striding by, a few leading prancing dogs, pulling at their leashes as though flaunting their unblemished motor skills.

As we sat, enjoying the late-afternoon light and the blessed company of the similarly afflicted, someone began singing. A cheerful male voice filled the concourse, echoing through the hushed space like the midnight song of a solitary bird:

Hey, hey, good lookin'
Whatcha got cookin'?
How's about cookin'
Somethin' up with me?

Turning, I spotted the song's source: a white-haired gentleman wearing a brown jacket. Head thrown back, face euphoric, he sat in a wheelchair, propelling himself forward with one leg and one arm.

"Hey," I said, as he passed us in full voice. "Thanks for your cheerful song."

He stopped and gave a cherubic grin. "You don't mind me cluttering up your air with my rusty voice?"

"Absolutely not," I replied.

"Good," he said. Giving the wheel a crank, and taking a "step" forward, he threw his head back, launched into the next verse, and continued his journey.

I've seen Christ in the halls of the hospitals we've visited recently. Sometimes I think I've seen his back, disguised as an old man pinching his nightgown shut as he wanders, looking for assistance to return to bed.

Sometimes I've heard his voice, sobbing and pleading for something to ease excruciating pain.

Sometimes I've seen his hands, gently guiding the Preacher's body into a more comfortable position or rubbing lotion on his skin, skin that's peeling like the outer layers of an onion as a result of an extremely high fever.

And at least once I'm sure I've heard him singing through the lips of someone profoundly grateful for what remains:

Hey, hey, good lookin'
Whatcha got cookin'?
How's about cookin'
Somethin' up with me?

I learned the singer's name only later. Archie McPeek has been in the centre thirteen years, and everywhere he goes, he sings. He knows all the words to all the songs of the fifties, and his voice and smile invite all within earshot to smile and sing, too.

I do, in fact. Every time we meet, Archie and I sing a duet. He looks up at me, and I sing the words I know, no matter who is listening.

Archie's pirate was a monster that attacked his brain. Here's the funny thing: Before Archie's tumours turned their lives upside down, Archie never sang. Not a note. His wife, Gail, says she doesn't know where the music came from, the voice, the repertoire ... the blessings.

I do.

Thursday, October 4

Rick is still a big man, but his forty-pound loss is most apparent in his narrowed face. When he takes his shirt off, his left shoulder reminds me of the photos of the concentration camp survivors. The other day I caught him lying on his back, turning his head from side to side.

"What are you doing?" I asked.

"Looking for muscles," he said sadly.

I spoke to Rick today day about his depression, trying to help him not feel guilty for the black cloud over him. I don't know if I was successful or not.

Rick had no therapy this afternoon, but felt so miserable after lunch that he wanted only to rest.

While he slept, I walked the mile or so around Wascana Lake. The sky was blue and the trees gold, and ducks and geese bobbed, tails up.

Today I saw a man dressed as a ship's captain, sailing remote controlled sailboats. Sometimes I see young canoeists learning their art. I enjoy it all: the fountains gaily splashing, the babies in their strollers, children's cheerful calls, the mosaic of leaves strewn across the browning grass.

But whenever I shuck the cloak of nurturing and feel a little pleasure, I feel guilty.

Tonight the plan was for me to cut Rick's hair before his bath. But he was too cold to sit in the sheets while I cut, so he had the bath only. A mistake, we realized in retrospect. The transfer to the bath chair itself brought on nausea, and the chair exacerbated it. Extreme nerve pain in his legs and an accidental mishandling of that wounded left shoulder brought him to the point of tears.

He shut his eyes tightly and said nothing for the entire bath, just trying to deal with the pain.

Friday, October 5
Thanksgiving weekend
E-mail Update

Hello, All,

Forgive me my humanity. At times, my positive attitude dissolves. What if we never do return from this physical and emotional place of exile? I ask myself sometimes. What if there are no more Thanksgiving hikes in the country, lakeside — or any side — vacations, overnight sleeps with the grandbeans, no more overnight sleeps side by side for that matter? What if we've seen the last company dinner, performed the last wedding, led our last congregation, lived in our last parsonage?

What if the pirates stole it all, after all? What then?

And on the fortieth day after the pirates of the West Nile invaded our little boat, I spoke to Richard, saying, "Even in the scripture, God only sentenced his people to forty days of hard stuff. So where did we go wrong?"

And Richard spoke back to me thus, saying, "Honey, I need the water bottle."

And it came to pass. It always does, eventually.

Some really very good things happened this week. I mean spectacularly good.

Friends and family from near and far blessed us with their presence.

Rick stood for a total of seven minutes in the standing frame.

I found out we have some disability insurance on our small loan.

We laughed until we cried at a chapter from Shirley Jackson's book *Life Among the Savages.*

And May, a friend who lives here in Regina, took me grocery shopping. Rick was out of diet ginger ale, and I was out of fresh vegetables.

When she brought me home — because for me, home is wherever my husband is — and she saw his state of weariness, and heard about his difficult nights, she said, "You should read him that poem every night."

I knew which poem she meant. I had given it to her last summer when she was having a difficult time getting to sleep.

"I didn't bring it with me," I said.

She looked at me strangely. Then she began to recite it to Rick and me, by heart:

Our Shepherd's Good Night

Now I lay thee down to sleep,
So close your eyes, my tired sheep.
The morning flies on wings of prayer,
To those who trust, I'm always there.

Now I lay thee down to sleep,
My precious child, your life I keep.
Thou shall not toss, nor turn, nor sigh,
I slumber not, I reign on high.

Now I lay thee down to sleep,
Your loved ones, child, trust me to keep.
No evil frightens me, no night
So black it can put out my light.

Now I lay thee down to sleep,
Your worries, child, give me to keep.
Please let me hold tomorrow's dread,
And turn it into faith instead.

The reason May was surprised that I didn't know the poem was that I wrote it myself, a few years ago, and have given it to many friends and family.

Hearing May recite those words overwhelmed me. But the best part came next. Wrapping her arm around my waist, she began singing the poem to a tune she had composed herself.

Tears came before she finished. Two nurses, coming in to prepare Rick for bed, slowly backed out of the room.

Faith, still,
Kathleen and Rick

Saturday, October 6

Rick surprised me this morning. After a horrible day yesterday, he told me he had had a blessed night of peaceful sleep. When I arrived in his room, he had eaten, dressed, was sitting upright, wearing a positive expression and visiting with his new roommate, George Murphy. I felt I had my husband back.

⌒

We had music in the concourse this day. Two middle-aged brothers in white shirts and black pants played accordion and guitar and sang old-time popular hits.

Two middle-aged women, one a resident, the other either her guest or a staff member, danced in front of the large lake mural to the song "Red Sails in the Sunset." A man without legs sat, impassive, but stayed for the entire concert. Two men tapped their good hands on the wheelchair arms; those with feet to move, moved them.

⌒

The nurse told us Rick's weight today: under 250. He has lost almost seventy pounds.

Sunday, October 7
Thanksgiving Day

A miracle, I think. Rick feels well for the second day running! And we are so thankful. How appropriate that this turnabout has occurred on this Thanksgiving weekend.

The chapel overflowed filled with people today. They came by foot and wheel. People like us, thankful for what remains. I left inspired by these phrases in two hymns of gratitude:

And keep us in his grace,
And guide us when perplexed,

And free us from all ills
In this world and the next.

...

For the wonders that astound us,
For the truths that will confound us,
Most of all that love has found us,
Thanks be to God!

This weekend has brought several batches of visitors from near and far. Some cried, as others have done, at the shock of seeing Rick so incapacitated. If only they could see how great his capacity has become.

Some brought cheer and chocolate and fruit and a whiff of the fragrance of the body of Christ. It was like a piece of us returned to us.

Some brought flowers, some their dog, and others homemade cookies, but they all brought the kind of encouragement we needed, particularly the sense that we are not forgotten, that we are still of value. Don and Dorothy Goings, dear Alberta friends who have ceaselessly encouraged us, have returned several times, bringing cheer each time.

Tonight Rick garnered another win in the ongoing Battle of the Bowels. We celebrated by offering some of our chocolate-covered almonds to all the attendees involved, the nurses and aides, and we laughed as if at a party.

Today Rick's mind is clear of the pirates' black flags and his body free of pain — or relatively so. A few twinges, charley horses, shoulder shudders ... but nothing like the all-out war we had on Friday.

On that day, his pain became so severe that no painkiller would touch it. Several nurses hovered around his bed, perplexed. Suzanne, one of the therapist's assistants, summoned from the OT department, even climbed up on his bed to manipulate his legs, in hopes of alleviating his discomfort.

Finally Arlene, the day's charge nurse, called a pharmacist. When she described his pain as nerve pain, he recommended another medication,

Gabapentin, instead of the morphine he's been taking. She called the doctor immediately, and the medication arrived within hours.

People were praying, and God answered. Today I have my husband back.

Tuesday, October 9

For the fourth day running, Rick had a relatively painless night and day, astounding the therapists and nurses who hadn't seen him since Friday.

"Who's this man with you?" one asked, her expression a comical blend of disbelief and relief.

Arlene was working this morning. Last Friday she said she wasn't going home until Rick smiled. This morning she cried in the hall when he gave her not only a smile, but a chuckle, as well.

During all three of his therapies, he charged through with the determination of an athlete. When we got back to the ward after the last session, he even told the nurses that the therapy felt *good*. They left his room shaking their heads, amazed.

Who but God could arrange this?

Thursday, October 11

At clinic today, Rick's "Dream Team" sat with us and discussed Rick's progress on his goals. Today everyone from the doctor on down was smiling. Rick, too, as he told them that his gloom is lifting, and that by next week he feels he'll be ready to be lifted in the piece of equipment he dreaded most back in Yorkton: the sit/stand lift.

He has been standing for seventeen minutes, well supported, in the standing frame, strengthening the leg and back muscles considerably. He's also able to roll onto his left side, from his back, and back again. The staff are almost as joyful as we are.

We've been marking half portions on all Rick's menus, and they've been quite sufficient. Tonight his supper was a quarter of a baked potato, and a quarter piece of ham. Poor man looked at it rather sadly. Still, he wouldn't let me make him extra.

"I don't want to gain back all the weight I've lost," he said.

I gave him a cookie at bedtime. He didn't refuse that.

⌒

We attended a concert in the concourse tonight by an Elvis impersonator billed as Gilvis. I had more fun watching the residents than listening to his singing. They sang along and danced in their wheelchairs (pushed by staff).

The entire remaining body of the man with no legs swayed in time with the music. A youth on a respirator smiled so hard his face almost disappeared. Two mentally challenged women held hands and giggled. Rick tapped his feet, nodded his head.

Friday, October 12

Rick stood for just past twenty minutes in the standing frame today. And Errin tried something new: electric therapy to help the muscles in his left shoulder tighten back up, so they can hold the bones together. She attached electrodes to the top of his shoulder, and another set to the top of his arm, then turned on the electrical current, which she says stimulates the muscles to contract in a simulation of their natural activity.

She left the electrodes on his shoulder for twenty minutes while she worked with another patient. I watched Rick wince as the skin on his arm jumped every few seconds with every new jolt.

⌒

Pedro is an ASS, and he's been one for four years. Pedro works here. "Love my job, but not the acronym," he told me today. ASS stands for Adaptive Seating Specialist. I've seen him often about the place, usually with tool in hand, hovering over someone's wheelchair.

Rick's chair needed a few adjustments, so we visited Pedro in his main-floor workspace, a cavernous concrete-floored shop, strewn with wheelchairs and wheelchair parts, rolls of canvas, and large, noisy equipment. He ushered us into a side-room for a consult.

"What can I do for you today?" he asked, crouching beside Rick's chair, ready to make his examination.

Rick listed all the things he wanted fixed: the back's leaning too far, the footrests are uneven, the cushion keeps slipping ...

"Anything more?" Pedro's face turned upward.

Rick shook his head and retreated to his quiet zone, but I chatted with Pedro while he worked.

I learned that after first being employed here as a shipper and receiver, he migrated into his job as an apprentice. It took three years for him to become a fully qualified ASS.

Now he spends his days assembling and adapting wheelchairs and other therapeutic aids to make disabled people's lives easier. The money's nice, he says. But I can tell there's more. Pedro truly cares. I've seen it in his expression as he crouches beside the chairs of people like Rick: people whose legs are round, with rubber and spokes, and whose hearts are often mangled and full of perplexity.

"You're helping people put their lives together, you know, Pedro."

"If I can help someone, that's what I like."

⌒

Maggie has been teaching me to help Rick transfer from bed to chair and back. When we can do that regularly, we won't need the lift. She praised my "form" today.

"Nice straight back," she said. "You didn't lose your position once."

Here's what this looks like:

Take the side arm off the wheelchair. Bend low in front of him, wrap my arms about his waist, do a lunge, front knee bent, back straight; brace legs, rock both our bodies back and forth, and then, on the count of three, HEAVE!

I never thought I'd be able to do it, but my husband's (still quite large) body slides neatly across the sliding board (a sturdy wide board tucked under his bottom) and lands on the surface to which he's transferring.

Following therapy this afternoon, we headed toward the elevators for his room — but turned back to listen to Bus playing piano in the concourse.

I can always tell when Bus is at the keyboard. The man's music soars to the glass roof, joins the sunshine, and becomes the spirit of optimism itself. Then it rains back down and washes over us, healing things that only music can heal.

We've heard him before, usually on Wednesdays. He makes that mellow brown piano rock with his unmistakable, impeccable renditions of old wartime songs. But he doesn't stop there — he also plays many of the jazz and pop songs that accompanied the healing post-war years.

Some days people sit and listen, as we do. And some days, no one does. That doesn't stop him.

"I play extra firmly then," he said, "because I know they can hear me on the wards, and some can't come out, but they enjoy it."

When we first met Bus, he finished playing, got up from the piano, and came over to where we sat.

"Bus Hillyard," he said, holding out his hand. "Hill and yard, just like it sounds."

Tall, graceful, and a World War II vet, Bus, well past eighty, has been coming here on Monday, Wednesday, and Friday, for fourteen years now. He began while visiting a good friend, a patient on the veteran's ward. The two had soldiered together, but his friend had been badly injured. When Bus visited, he played the piano.

Then his friend died. Sorrowing, Bus stopped coming. But the centre's administration phoned him one day. "People are asking about you," they told him. So he returned. Played again, just as he had always done, and hasn't stopped since.

Monday, October 15

Exhaustion set in today, replacing the exhilaration of the last week's highs. We managed each activity, but everything drained us completely. It felt as though we were strapped to a hand plow, and breaking new ground. For the first time in this saga of suffering, I asked myself, and God, "When will it end?"

That's a dangerous question. Because there are many things about this experience I don't want to end. I don't want the closeness Rick and I feel to end. The "being yoked together," pulling toward the same end.

I don't want the simplicity of this life to end. The bare concrete room I sleep in doesn't have much by way of aesthetics, but it has everything I need: a place to lay my weary body at the end of each day, a window with a view, a bathroom, a phone, a desk, and a closet. What more could one really want?

I'm strangely spoiled here. In a sense, life is easy. I don't have to clean a house. Staff come into my hostel room to vacuum and clean my shower and toilet. I make the bed, but they'd do that, too, if I let them. I don't have to fetch meals for anyone except myself.

Most of my writing deadlines have vanished. I don't feel pressured to answer e-mails, to write stories, to teach classes, to play the piano, to answer a phone. I have no leaves to rake, no garden to clean, no lawn to mow.

I don't want the sense of intimacy with Christ to end. This circumstance has brought me closer to him than I've been in a very long time.

"You should take time for devotions," May told me, alarmed one day when I explained how full our day is of scheduled activities, and mine with caring for Rick, and how tired I am when I finally get back here to my room.

I laughed. The notion of spending only fifteen minutes with God seems ludicrous.

Sometimes I feel as though God has dumped me inside a devotional book, and not a nice one at that. For a time, we have been privileged to share in the sufferings of Christ. It has been horrible; it has been sublime.

Of course I want Rick's pain to end, but in some inexplicable way this journey down West Nile has brought us both closer to our Father. Knowing that we are made of the same raw human material as the ancient, faithless Israelites, I genuinely dread the seemingly inevitable cooling of our faith when life isn't so much of a struggle. I don't want the feeling of being close to the stuff that makes people human to end. The sufferings of our fellow patients and their families. The music that floats us through our days, usually streaming from people who know well what it is to be lonely and suffering, and who freely share their gifts. The sight of broken bodies making do, fighting back, simply surviving, serving anyway, and being served humbly.

I don't want to lose the fresh sense of what it means to be part of God's family. The reminder that we matter, not only to God but to so many others, as well. The overwhelming flood of support, which like the multitudes of relief workers who swarm to each global disaster, can't last, though it will always linger in our hearts.

I don't want to lose the beautiful, singular focus that envelops my days. All the flotsam and jetsam and accumulated detritus of two too-crowded lives have been swept aside as though by a tsunami. All that remains is doing whatever it takes to restore Rick to health.

⌒

He stood in the standing frame for fifteen minutes today. After his afternoon therapy, I rolled him outside to enjoy the dwindling autumn. We took the back way to Spruce Island, out on the lake. The trip included rather a lot of jiggling of that poor left arm.

At the lake, we saw the broken-winged goose I'd seen earlier, still trying to fatten up for a flight it may never take.

Tuesday, October 16

The Bean laughed me goodnight over the phone tonight. He wanted me to join him in "Heimer Schmidt." So, as staff came in and out of Rick's room, I sang:

"John JacobJingleheimer Schmidt,
His name is my name too.
Whenever we go ..." And here I paused ...

"*OUT,*" said the Bean, two hundred kilometers away.
"*The people always ...*"
"*SHOUT,*" the Bean chorused.
"*John JacobJingleheimer Schmidt!*"
"*Na, na, na, na, na, na, na ... NA!*" we finished together.

The Bean rained giggle after giggle through the phone receiver. I thought he was laughing at the song, until Amanda told me she'd been tickling him so I could hear his laughter. Her thoughtfulness moves me.

Amanda must be growing quite round now. I sometimes forget that another wee one is waiting at the gate to charm and steal our hearts, just as its older siblings have.

Wednesday, October 17

Rick stood today, outside the standing frame. First Errin put a physio belt on him (a wide nylon belt that gives the therapists something to hang on to), raised the physio bed until only his toes touched the floor, and placed a raised wheeled table called a plinth in front of him. Two assistants, Pat and Suzanne, stood watch, like guardian angels, one on the opposite side of Errin, and one at Rick's back.

I watched him scoot, using a combination of feet and butt cheeks, to the edge of the therapy bed. The therapists each took hold of his physio belt, around his waist, and gave the count ... one, two, three ... and hefted him up. He stood swaying like a tall ship in the wind sometimes, but mostly he stood standing sermon straight, as each therapist supported or guarded his knees or his back.

The girls gave a running commentary:

This knee is out a little; bring it in, Rick. Slide this hip over a little, shoulders back, are you meaning to lean a little? Did you just do that, or was it an accident? (This when his knee moved out of Pat's protective hold, all by itself.) How do you feel, how do you feel *now*, how did that just feel, are you feeling queasy ... shoulders back, you're tilting ... come on back over to my side a little, can you move this leg out just a little ...

RICK STOOD TODAY!

Another astounding thing happened. A friend visited, bringing the last month's mail from home. I began sorting and opening the business mail first. Each envelope reminded me that beyond these walls is a world that clamours for attention, where bills need paying, choices need making, commitments need keeping. A world, according to the pictures in the few flyers that had somehow gotten into the rest of the mail, for people with legs and arms that do what they're supposed to. An expensive world.

I tried to stop thinking about these realities as I opened our bills. Tried not to remember the rent we owed for my hostel room, or our increased bills and decreased income.

"Let's open the personal mail," I said to Rick.

I picked up a small envelope first. We noted the return name and address as that of a woman we barely know and haven't seen for years, perhaps decades. Inside the envelope was a green half sheet of paper with a note and the words to an old hymn.

She wanted to send this gift anonymously, her note said, but had to write a cheque because she couldn't get the cash in the envelope.

God had impressed on her heart a specific amount he wanted her to give, she said. She had tried to argue with him — and I could picture a grin — but nevertheless was obedient.

"No phone calls to thank me, please," she wrote.

I didn't look at the cheque until after I had read the note aloud to Rick. When I did, my eyes blurred. I rubbed them, blinked again, and once more tried to read the amount on the cheque, sure I must have got it wrong. The amount astounded us.

Then Rick said, softly, "I don't remember much about her, but I believe she is also disabled now."

I felt my face crumple like a dry leaf in a child's hand. I cried at the marvel of God's faithfulness. I cried at our own unworthiness. I cried at the generosity of an understanding heart. I cried for the miracle of the broken helping the broken. And then I read the words to the hymn on the other side of the note:

Be not dismayed, whate'er betide,
God will take care of you ...

Thursday, October 18

Some of the people we've met here — patients and their families as well as staff — are beginning to find us, to ask for prayer, or simply to sit and talk. Hurting people who long for a safe place to let things out. I'm ever conscious that sometimes it's the small things, the one-minute opportunities that can change a life forever. I long not to waste those opportunities.

On the ward this morning I greeted one of the nurses as she passed us in the hall. She's taken care of Rick a few times, and we've shared some special memories of India. It's her native country, and she is fascinated that I have spent time there. Today she looked extra tired and I told her so.

She looked at me with the innocence of a child, and said, with a frankness I recall so well in her compatriots, "I'm going through a very hard time just now."

Then, like a little bird come home, this lovely Hindu lady actually leaned into my side. In what seemed a particularly busy moment there in front of the nursing station, I wrapped one arm around her shoulder. She laid her head on my shoulder and I kissed her cheek.

"I'm so sorry," I said. "I'll pray for you."

"That's what I need," she said fervently. "That's what I need."

This morning in our six-pack David spoke about God being his strength in the middle of messes.

Like David, I, too, pray often: *Father, my Strength, my Hope.*

The words resonate in me. I wake up singing them; I go to bed remembering them, often too tired to voice them; and sometimes when the night surrounds like blackstrap molasses, I whisper them until the light returns.

Friday, October 19

Standing in the frame, surrounded by Errin and another therapist, Rick began heel-toeing his foot forward and back a few inches. And out to the side a few inches, though he told me later he had cheated, locking his knees in order to perform that feat. Small steps, but truly giant ones, encouraging to him and the therapists.

After lunch I left Rick at OT so I could do some banking.

May picked me up and dropped me off downtown where all three of our banks are a mere few steps from each other. I had donned my fake leather jacket and tucked my limp hair behind my ears. It's much in need of a wash, but I got up early this morning to write a column and didn't leave enough time for my already severely curtailed "beauty routine." No clean hair, no makeup, and one large pimple on my left cheek. I'm not lovely, but all my parts work, and that's beautiful to me.

In the Cornwall Centre, people zigged and zagged around me. Halloween is two weeks hence, but some stores are already decorated for Christmas.

One store had a plethora of Christmas trees, lit and decorated, posed among witches and goblins and orange pumpkins.

I felt no emotion except surprise that I felt no emotion. No excitement, no sadness, simply detachment. This world is not my home.

Friday, October 19
E-mail Update

Family, Friends, and All,

At Wednesday's clinic, Rick, surrounded by his practitioners, sat tall in his wheelchair. Eyes open, totally responsive. Completely (praise God!) pain free.

Some in that circle had difficulty believing this to be the same man I had wheeled into that room a few weeks ago.

Once more the Dream Team did a thorough review of Rick's goals. He's making progress in every area, sitting, standing. In fact, in his supported stands (out of the frame now, but surrounded by therapists, like guardian angels), he's begun slightly shifting his weight from side to side and inching each foot forward and back.

New things this week: He began using a sliding board to transfer himself from chair to bed and reverse on his good side. The people crane has moved on to find another bag of relief goods.

This week he can even get that stubborn left arm to balance on its elbow for a few seconds before it flops forward — or backward or sideward. He almost gave himself a black eye flicking it about in bed the other night. His fist flopped backward before he could catch it. His glasses saved him.

"How are you doing with 'sit to lie and lie to sit'?" someone asked.

"I can go down, no problem," he said.

Someone passed around a delectable bar of the darkest kind of exotic chocolate laced with coffee grounds. Rick, coffee hater, refused. But I broke off a piece and ate it. It felt like celebration.

I can tell we have something to celebrate: He's getting bossy again. This can only mean that a deliberate bid for independence lies immediately ahead.

"Can't you make this wheelchair go straight?" he asks repeatedly. He never did like my driving.

I tell him it's because he's lighter on one side than the other now. He's not buying it.

Finally, I say, "Hey you, I take you where you need to go. I don't complain, and I don't charge you. Plus, my legs work and yours don't. So enough already."

He has decided to like my driving.

Seriously, God has dramatically sped up the progress we've seen to this point. (We've told him all along we wouldn't mind if he wanted to do that.) Rick's legs won't hold him up to walk yet, but he can slide his feet along the floor. Helped by his good right hand, he can make his own wheelchair move.

This afternoon I had to go downtown to do some banking. When he thought I had been gone long enough, he "walked" his own wheelchair down the hall outside his room. Then he rolled himself into the elevator and down to main floor, where he waited in the concourse.

When I didn't return soon enough, he rolled himself back up to his room. He was utterly exhausted when I did return, but quite pleased with himself. That bid for independence? This was it, I think.

We have a new goal, Rick and I, and it's well on its way to fulfillment. It is this: to discover, when all this is over, that when they boarded our little boat, the pirates of the West Nile left us with more treasure than they took.

What treasure have we already found? Strength for today, hope for tomorrow, again and again. Shared time of the highest quality; laughter and tears as we reach for common goals; walking (rolling), reading, visiting together. An intensely focused life.

We're experiencing the joy of seeing God from a new angle as we daily (several times daily) enjoy reading scripture and praying together. The fascination of watching the workings of this healing place from the inside out. The immense privilege of sharing in others' sufferings and praying for and with them. Music over the West Nile.

And perhaps the most moving and surprising treasure: the tremendous updraft of love and support we feel from our friends and family and God's family, even from some who are total strangers.

Through you, God has provided everything we've needed, each day, thus far, and over and above that on many days. We'll never be able to thank you adequately, so instead we pray that God blesses you as you've blessed us.

So, knowing what we know now, what would we do if we could go back in time and relive the occasion of the mosquito bite? I can't answer for Rick. No amount of treasure can diminish the impact of his physical pain and losses. And even though we have hope for recovery, we have no guarantees of what the days ahead will hold. ("We see you improving," Dr. Yip told us yesterday. "But we have no idea whether that will carry on, or whether you'll plateau and remain at a fixed point.")

No, the answer to that question will be Rick's alone when we've landed on the other side of West Nile. But we know this: The simple act of trusting our Father to provide strength for each day and hope for each tomorrow has been healing in and of itself. Spiritually healing.

"Do not worry about tomorrow," Jesus said, to those he knew were fretting about the necessities of daily life. "Each day has enough trouble of its own" (Matthew 6:34). He also promised to provide what we need when we make it our habit to follow him.

And so we decide each day not to bargain or assume or play the shoulda, woulda, coulda game. This is the way our river has run. But Jesus is in our little boat. His presence reminds us that he can calm storms (even those on the West Nile) or bolster us through the storm until its rage becomes a gentle sea breeze that wafts us home. And we are grateful, and still not disappointed.

Thank you all for your love. We, and God, love you right back. And daily we pray for your own little boats, wherever your river of life finds you. Take Jesus along.

Cheers,
Kathleen and Rick

Sunday, October 21

Someone cancelled the in-house church service today. So instead, I rolled Rick out to the bench at the front of the hospital to read our six-pack. The sun shone, but the wind had bad breath, as though it had tasted winter, and my hands turned the pages stiffly. But Rick, bundled only in his prayer shawl, didn't mind, so I began reading.

We hadn't gotten very far when two people who had been sitting on the other side of the entryway at a corresponding bench got up and moved over to our side, where the wind wasn't as strong.

We carried on without stopping, but when we were done, we chatted with both of them. The woman, an obvious cancer patient, with little extra flesh and hair just beginning to return, told us she was staying at the hostel because her house was being gutted and repaired after an internal fire last summer.

On the day of the fire, she had been out taking treatments for a cancerous brain tumour, from which she should have died, or so it sounds, a long while ago.

"I was looking forward to retiring from my job soon," she said wryly. "I'm going to — or was going to — take up a second career in real estate."

The young man, a swarthy fellow with his leg in a cast, likely in his thirties, sat in his wheelchair.

"What landed you in this chair?" I asked.

"A relative ran me over," he said simply.

"On purpose?" I said before I could catch myself.

He shrugged. "We don't know."

Oh God, preserve us from pirates, from monsters and madmen and beasts.

⌒

The children arrived around four. We met them in the concourse.

I pray that in years to come, when these particular Beans are adults and have no time for the likes of us, they will remember this day, simply for the joy of it. Gampa in a wheelchair; their own rides around the ward in that wheelchair; eating roommate George's fish dinner at a bedside table from a tray just like Gampa's (George has gone home for the weekend, but his tray arrived anyway); snuggling up to Gampa in bed; running, running down the long wide ribbon of hallways; riding in the elevators and pressing the wrong button and setting off the alarm.

I hope Benjamin will recall the courtyard playground where he and I swung side by side: he securely in a gray rubber child's swing, and I in a "chair" swing.

Mid-swing, he noticed a Canadian flag that had been placed in one of the hostel windows.

"Flag," he said, pointing.

"That's a Canadian flag, Benjamin," I said. "Canada is our country. We all live in Canada."

I got off my swing to push him again, and in rhythm began to chant, "Benjamin lives in Canada, Nana lives in Canada, Gampa lives in Canada, Mama lives in Canada, Daddy lives in Canada, Tabatha lives in Canada ..."

He began to laugh, high and merry, and I went on.

"Grandma lives in Canada, great-grandma lives in Canada ..."

His peals were so merry that I began laughing, too, and so we laughed together, my biggest Bean and I.

"Canada, Canada, Canada," he echoed, gasping for air.

Inside, we played under a large rainbow that arches over the waiting room at the children's clinic. Tabatha contented herself with opening and closing the door to the children's house, and Benjamin moved coloured beads around on a standing wire frame.

Moved by what, I don't know — most likely the rainbow over us — I began singing:

Somewhere over the rainbow, way up high ...

Benjamin suddenly left his beads, straightened himself to a standing position, and looked at me, his great blue eyes filled with wonder. But with something else, too: ineffable sadness. Lost memories perhaps?

Whispers of sunny summer days when he and I walked and talked alone, listening to birds singing and watching the trees dance — those must seem so very far behind him.

Shadowed memories of days we splashed in mud puddles, walked together to the construction site, our hands swinging; of afternoons we dug holes in the garden with neighbour Lorraine's toy excavator.

Days when we slid down slides and rolled down hills and did all the things grandmothers are supposed to do with their little grandchildren.

Or maybe it was none of that.

Without taking his eyes off me, he said softly, but with great emphasis, as though pronouncing an infallible truth: "Dat's my fav-it song!"

SUNNY SIDE UP
October 31

Hope, Like Stars in the Dark

On the day we moved in, Jen's wheelchair spun out of the room next to the Preacher's. I recall two thoughts: "She's so young!" And, "She's enjoying herself!"

Up on the third floor of the rehab centre where Rick and I live these days, she was the first fellow patient I recall seeing. Laughter, I thought. In this place? In that chair?

I looked again. Early twenties, I guessed. Pencil-thin arms. Short brown hair, neatly styled. Glasses. Lovely skin. And a smile and laugh that rolled down the hall faster than her speeding wheelchair, propelled by friend power.

Jennifer Gabrysh, we found out later, took a dive while swimming last summer and exploded a few critical bones in her spine. Her resulting spinal cord injury has ensured her a seat — her own wheelchair — at all public and private functions, perhaps for the rest of her life. Or so some say. She doesn't believe it.

On the day he was wheeled in here, immobilized by West Nile disease, the Preacher saw Jen, too. But I wouldn't know how deeply our first glimpse of this young woman had affected him until weeks later.

"I would like to talk to Jen," he told me when we heard her cheerful voice passing in the hallway one evening. "Can you see if she'll come in here?"

I stepped into the doorway. Jen and a friend were already halfway down the hall, but I called her back, wondering what she would think: We had not progressed past the occasional

"Hi" en route to or during therapy sessions.

Jen and her friend came in gladly. We chatted awhile, then the Preacher said, "Jen, you won't remember this, but when I came in here, scared and feeling hopeless, I noticed you. At the time I was so discouraged, but your spirit shone. It seemed you were the only one smiling. You gave me hope and bolstered my faith. I'll always remember that. I just wanted to thank you."

Jen sat quietly in her chariot at the foot of his bed.

"Every day, Jen," I added, "we ask God to send strength for that day, and hope for tomorrow. You were his messenger of hope that day."

Jen, seeming almost embarrassed, humbly explained how God keeps sending her hope, too, in small bite-sized packages: insightful devotional readings, friends, worship services at various churches.

Her hope is simple: that one day she'll prove the experts wrong and abandon her chair forever.

I've learned something during these months since the pirates of the West Nile invaded the Preacher's and my little boat: that we need darkness. All of us.

Because only in the blackest of nights can we find the stars that God has meticulously set in place to help lead us home.

Saturday, October 27

I have a large purse, and it began ringing this morning in Rick's room. I rummaged inside for the cell phone, but couldn't find it. After about fifteen rings, it stopped.

Suddenly a voice emerged from the bottom of the purse. "Hello? Mom? Are you there?"

Amanda's voice. I panicked and started yelling at my purse: "Amanda! Hello! Don't hang up!"

"Mom?"

"Yes, I hear you, but I can't find you!"

"What do you mean, you can't find me?"

"You're in my purse somewhere, honey, but I can't find you. Now I'm afraid that if I keep looking, I'll do something to cut you off and you'll disappear, so I'll just have to stand here talking to my purse."

From deep inside dark brown leather and the type of clutter only found in women's purses — wallets, Kleenex (new and used), books, pens, notepads — I heard only laughter.

For the rest of our conversation, I simply bent my head over my open purse, listening and talking. The ward was quiet, as it always is on Saturdays, and Rick's roommate had checked out for the weekend.

If anyone walked past our room, they would have witnessed my conversation with my purse. I didn't notice if they did, being rather busy at the time. Rick, too, who was enjoying this Wascana version of *Get Smart*.

I found the phone after the purse said goodbye. Still neatly closed. Think I'll put that purse on eBay.

Thursday, November 1
E-mail Update

Dear All,

This morning I remained in my room writing a tad too long. Around nine, a brisk knock interrupted me. Rick. He can, though slowly, roll himself almost anywhere in the building now. The effort exhausts him, but he's stronger than he was several weeks ago.

His left arm has gained strength, too, though that shoulder took another few hits later in the week (from working it too hard) and dislocated again. This has been a frequent occurrence, and sets him back whenever it happens. So he's back to wearing his shoulder harness, the foam rubber and Velcro contraption designed by Maggie, his occupational therapist, to keep the bones in place. But he has more control over the forearm, and the dexterity in the left-hand fingers is improving.

The Beans visited on Thursday and saw that firsthand.

They accompanied Rick to OT and watched him use his left hand to put together (or attempt to) a giant wooden puzzle, turn wing nuts onto a board of bolts, and muck around with Thera-putty.

The children were especially interested in the putty.

"Would you like to play with it?" Maggie asked.

Benjamin accepted the pile of moldable yellow rubber carefully. Hesitating at first, he began digging his fingers in and drawing them forward, just like Gampa.

Looking up, his eyes met mine. "Not poo, Nana," he said reassuringly. "Is not poo."

Amanda and I figured it out: He had never heard the word putty before. Likely "potty" was the closest he could find in his two-year-old vocabulary.

~

Her friend wheeled her over to where I sat at the piano trying to play "Somewhere Over the Rainbow," without the music. Rick sat beside me in his wheelchair, and that's how we met Norma.

I don't play much without music. That's Rick's department. I need notes, for most songs. Words and chords at least. Something black on a white page. I panic when I'm forced to wing it in church. But we were alone. No audience to criticize. The centre's large concourse echoed with my attempts.

Void of traffic, the vast hall's freshly polished floors awaited tomorrow's onslaught of wheelchair tires and shoe heels. Every note I played echoed from the solarium roof that rose high and black above us:

Someday I'll wish upon a star,
And wake up where the clouds are far behind me ...

It's serious business, this wheelchair existence. Norma, an MS victim, mother of two young adults, has lived here for six years. Not only can she not walk, but her hands don't function well enough to maneuver her chair. She propels herself by blowing puffs of air into a mouth tube positioned near her face, then pressing directional buttons on a small screen in front of her.

Unless a friend is nearby. Then she puts the chair into neutral so the friend can push from behind.

But that's not all we learned about Norma that night under the dark concourse.

Both Norma and her friend are Christians. Norma told us she believes God has a plan for her, but she can't figure it out yet. God has kept her alive for a reason, and she's content to wait to discover it.

The friend, however, told us that she believes God wants to miraculously release Norma from her chair and will do so on the day she's able to muster enough faith. She wishes she had enough of the stuff to release Norma herself, but openly admits that she doesn't.

"I'm not brave enough," she said. "I wish I was, but I can't do it yet."

It's a popular notion, and a pervasive one, propagated by all too many well-known teachers and preachers who seem to have ignored huge chunks of scripture and by the ill-taught who sit on pews and couches lapping up their teachings: the notion that chronic illness (and poverty) is never God's will for believers, and is caused and maintained by a lack of faith. That those with the right quality and/or amount of faith can, by invoking the right words, manipulate God into making them healthy, wealthy, and wise.

Just like how Norma maneuvers her chair. A little puff of faith will get you going, and a large puff (if you can manage it) along with exactly the right spoken words, recited repeatedly like a mantra, will propel you past the next pillar and clear out of the building.

"For six years, you've lived in that chair, Norma," I said. "You've been confined in the worst sort of bodily prison, and yet you love and trust God. To us, that's a much greater testimony of God's power than an instant miracle."

Norma cried.

Her friend pursed her lips. Said (with more than a little ice frosting her voice), "I believe differently."

A few minutes later, she wheeled Norma away. But not before Norma told us this: "I heard the piano in my room and wanted to come out here to listen to the woman who often comes here to play hymns. Instead, God wanted me to meet you."

"Or perhaps it was so we could meet you," I told her.

Love,
Kathleen and Rick

Saturday, November 3

This afternoon we wandered downstairs and parked ourselves opposite the windows beside the third courtyard where Rick could see out. I got comfortable in one of the orange tweed chairs and took out my old laptop to write. After about half an hour, the strains of a Saturday-afternoon flute and guitar concert wafted down the concourse. Rick began walking his chair toward the sound, and I started packing up my computer to join him.

Just then the man in the red wheelchair wheeled over. We say hello whenever we encounter this very disabled young man, but not much more. He's a long-term resident here. He seems to have no ability to talk, though he does bellow frequently. He stopped beside me and grunted, arms flailing and legs jerking. I had no idea what that grunt meant, but I greeted him back as I zipped up my case. Then, because we've really never tried to go farther than "Hi," I decided to try.

"Just tuckin' my computer away. I'm a writer, and this is a nice quiet place to write. I see you have something that looks like a computer on your chair. Do you like computers? What is that thing anyway?"

I moved closer for a better look.

I didn't learn anything about that computer, but under it I saw a laminated sheet of words. Many words. Suddenly I realized that inside his body, so different from mine, was someone entirely different, someone I yearned to meet. And here was the tool to help me find him.

"You can talk to me!" I said, almost shouting. "How do you feel today?"

He raised his left arm and threw it into the air. When it landed, his thumb slid over the board and finally stopped at a word that still astounds me: "Happy."

"What are you doing today?" I asked.

This time the thumb pointed to another word: "Music."

I assumed he was referring to the music in the concourse.

I had to leave to catch up to Rick, but I plan to find out more about this young man.

Sunday, November 4

Someone cancelled church again today. We took the long roll there, saw the sign, and returned to the vacant concourse, where we got out our hymnbook and sat playing hymns. Rick sang along on a few songs, and when I closed my book a half hour later, I noticed Don and Glenda sitting behind me.

"You're touching hearts here, I hope you know," Don said.

We're all a little more in tune with our hearts these days. My own is telling me something in a language it's never used before: Our talents are truly given for the good of others, not simply for ourselves.

⌒

I rolled Rick down to the lakeside again. I've noticed that people are friendlier when you're rolling someone in a wheelchair. It's a little like walking a puppy. Most people at least smile, and some say hello.

Rick tells me, though, that when he's rolling his own chair, most people look right through him. He has noticed that it's that way for others, too.

Tuesday, November 6

Craig. That's the name of the young man in the red chair.

Rick and I read our six-pack in the solarium as usual today. Just as we finished, Craig rolled over to see us. This time as we talked he tried to rip off the white keyboard, which is attached to his chair table with Velcro. I helped him, and noticed under it even more words.

He pointed to two words at the bottom of the laminated sheet. Craig Fisher.

"This is your name? Craig?"

He pumped his right arm up and down and made bellow-like sounds that we assumed were laughter.

"Come see my room," he thumbed.

"Okay," I said. "Let's go right now."

Rick had to go to physiotherapy, so I followed Craig into one of the ground-floor long-term rooms in a ward we've never entered. A nameplate on the door of the room at the very end read "Craig Fisher."

Craig wheeled himself in, then turned around and watched me. He's enjoying this, I realized. Enjoying seeing me discover him as a person, not merely a challenging body. I felt shame for my initial assumptions when I had seen him careering about in the concourse like a wheelchair madman. I assumed, as likely many do, that he was not only physically challenged but mentally, too.

In his room I saw: a high bed draped with a thick-fleece Canadian-flag blanket; an extensive CD library on a high shelf along one wall; posters of the like I've seen in most young men's rooms, of rock bands and movie stars; a stereo system and music keyboard or two; and a state-of-the-art computer with an e-mail open on the screen.

I couldn't help reading the e-mail: "Dad ... this recorder doesn't work. I need to send it back. Craig."

Too dumbfounded for words, too amazed to do anything at all, I stood as still as Lot's wife in the centre of Craig's world. Wondering that he had let me in, wondering what to do now.

A staff member mopping the floor rescued me. She told me to ask this amazing young man yes and no questions.

"If he raises his right arm, he means yes. His left arm means no."

As Craig and I talked, I felt something tearing in my spirit. A thick veil between my ability and his extra-ability. Between my cautious-ness and his adventurousness, my prejudice and his inclusiveness.

And through that magic thumb, I learned that this man in the challenging body is a high-school grad, thirty-three years old; that he has a website; that a few summers ago, he participated in a novel project called "Challenging Bodies," where together with his music therapist (on keyboard) he was able to use technology to perform and compose music for a public audience.

I learned something else. The white toy on his table isn't a toy at all. It's a wireless computer keyboard by which he surfs the web and send e-mails. Laborious tasks, but clearly ones he enjoys.

Of course he does. Craig's computer takes him places where his body can't: into the lives and hearts of those who may never give him a chance to tell them even as much as his name.

Before I left, Craig reached out and drew me in tightly with his right arm.

"Is that a hug?" I asked, not sure.

But I hugged him back anyway.

Wascana is a world apart from mine, but I'm beginning to find I like it here. God, champion of losers, are you smiling?

Thursday, November 8

The library is at the far end of the second floor of this vast complex. I usually push Rick there, but yesterday he decided to try to go without wife power. Walking his wheelchair and using his good right arm, he did. And made it back again, too, though his trip exhausted him.

At supper, I congratulated him on his adventurous spirit. I noticed something strange in his eyes as he shrugged off my praise.

Today, with a hint of guilt, he admitted something.

"Hon, I had fun yesterday," he said.

"Really? What kind of fun?"

"Let's go to the library, and I'll show you."

I wheeled him down the long run of sky-hall, the second floor hall that overlooks the concourse below and runs under the solarium for almost the entire length of this vast building.

The main part of the complex and the wing that houses the library were built in different eras. Somehow the hall of the main building ended up considerably higher than the add-on. A long ramp solves the problem.

"Stop," he said, when we reached the ramp's top end.

I did, and before I could wonder why, he was gone, his legs lifted a few inches off the floor, his right hand sliding along the handrail, his chair racing toward the wall at the bottom where the hall takes a sharp right turn into the library.

I watched in horror, certain of a splat, but just before he crashed, his grip closed on the handrail. His chair gave a mighty jerk, then disappeared around the corner.

I flew down that long ramp as fast as he had. He was waiting for me around the corner, grinning.

"What are you *thinking*," I said. "You're a crazy man! What if someone was coming around that corner? You only have one good arm, Rick. D'ya wanna lose that, too? And what if you missed and hit the wall? Did you think about that?

Unrepentant, still high from his whoosh, he sat there trying to stifle his smirk.

"I'm okay," he protested.

"Rick, *promise* me you'll never do that again. *Promise.* You must *never* do that again!"

He promised.

Friday, November 9

This morning, while reading our six-pack in the solarium, Rick made me read one of our psalms again, the one that referred to Moses as a priest.

"I've never noticed that before," he said, pondering. "Moses wasn't a priest, he was a leader. Aaron was the priest. I'll have to think on that."

I can't explain the tickle of delight I felt. Though he can't concentrate enough to read yet, we both hope he'll be able to return to his own reading and study of the book that has been his life (not to mention his livelihood).

Saturday, November 10

"I'm coming home in November, Mom," Anthony told me last month. He has returned from B.C. to live at home while he takes a month-long health/nutrition course in Yorkton. He makes the two-hour trip down to visit us here on weekends, and brings us fabulous food from home — vegetarian stews, whole grain bread, cornmeal butter. He cooked it in our own kitchen — the same one where I taught him to make pies as a teenager.

The lad can cook, and somehow escaped inheriting his father's baloopa gland. Rick complains that whenever a foreign object enters his mouth (that's almost everything except meat and potatoes and a few raw vegetables), it instantly baloopas out the same way it went in.

Today Anthony noticed on his dad's tray, beside his roast beef, a mound of horseradish. Rick offered it to him, chuckling as he reminded him of his first taste of that peppery root. As a boy, one night during a family dinner with friends, Anthony took an entire spoonful of the stuff, despite our warnings. His face began glowing red, his eyes became pools of pain, and I thought we were going to have to extinguish him.

That story reminded him of something.

"Ever had wasabi?" he asked.

I nodded.

"Did you like it?"

I nodded again.

"I hadn't, and I didn't," he said.

Then he told us about his first wasabi experience. He had helped himself to an entire spoonful and popped it into his mouth.

"My ears started ringing and my eyes started bleeding," he began.

I watched Rick as he listened to Anthony's story, his own eyes watering, his shoulders shaking.

The ability to make people laugh is one of our son's many gifts. So is a warm heart.

Today he spent time with Craig, treating him with deep respect and kindness.

I wonder what he felt, meeting our new friend for the first time, this locked-up individual only a few years older than he, and just as intelligent, I'm sure.

I had told Craig that Anthony has some expertise working with sound equipment. This morning he waited with us until Anthony arrived. We introduced them, and Craig, pointing to words and letters on his board, asked Anthony if he would help him get his new eight-track digital recorder working. Anthony agreed to try.

"Did this thing come with a manual?" Anthony asked Craig.

Out went Craig's arm, down came his thumb. J A P...

"Japanese?" Anthony said, and began to chuckle.

Craig caught his laughter and suddenly the two were laughing, bellowing, and snorting together, like any pair of friends working on a project.

Anthony managed to get the machine working. We did a test recording with our voices. I sang "John Jacob JingleHeimer," Craig bellowed, and Anthony said, "Test, test."

Saturday, November 10
E-mail Update

Dear Ones,

We can't escape the pirates. On October 31, as I headed down the staircase from my hostel room to main floor, I met one coming up: one of the nurses, nattily dressed in loosely gathered trousers, tapered to the ankles, billowing white shirt, and large black hat. It was Halloween, after all, so I took no offence at this particular member of the species.

During the same week at a book sale in the concourse, I found a book titled *Pirateology*, full of pirate trivia. When pirates of old raised a red flag, I read, it meant they intended to fight to the death for their treasure; that they would extend no quarter to those whose ships they invaded. But when they raised a black flag, it indicated that if their victims surrendered their treasures peacefully, they would grant mercy and leave them with their lives.

Have I mentioned the view from my room? Outside my third-floor window stands a tree. The tree, which until a few weeks ago was still sheathed in gold, stands guard over a children's playground. On that playground stands a play-structure loosely built to resemble a ship. Complete with a telescope, a captain's wheel, portholes, and a long curved gangplank.

But it was the sinister-looking flag flapping in the stiff September wind which made me tell God that, considering our situation, he might have restrained his sense of humour. Did he have to place the pirate ship right where I had to look at it every morning?

When I read that bit about pirate flags in the pirate trivia book, I realized something. The flag that daily flaps in the breeze on the ship beneath my window is black.

Mercy, if we surrender.

Though we (especially Rick) have struggled with pain and loss, depression and uncertainty, we've not fought back with burning anger, regret, or bitterness: Those attitudes would simply have made this journey all the more difficult. Perhaps it's that choice that has allowed God's mercy to flow in such abundance around our little boat.

What mercy? Every day we thank God for the gift of Rick's life. For the gift of our friends and family. For the gift of the staff who are God's hands extended in these healing halls. For the gift of this unique perspective on health, ability, and disability. For the gift of those we have met in this place. For the gift of startling new perspectives on God, life, disability, and faith.

In spite of the difficulty, in spite of the question marks that punctuate our days, and those ahead, we're having a good time. Honest.

A few "markers" this week:

Rick fell out of bed this week. Don't panic (though the nurses did). He was trying to get up to a sitting position on his bad side, reached over his body to push himself up with his right arm, and missed. The momentum of his roll landed him on the floor, half kneeling, half crouching.

Those knees haven't knelt for a very long time.

He says he managed to tug his pillow (call cord attached) down with his bad arm (which remained, stranded, on top of the bed) and his teeth. No, don't ask. I wasn't there to see.

When the nurses answered, he said, "Uh, I'm on the floor and I would like to get up, please."

Later, he told me he should have told them he had finished praying for them now, and would they please assist him back onto his chair?

I'm crying as I write this, so forgive any disjointed sentences. On Thursday, for the first time in seventy-nine days, Rick took his first steps. Not walking like you or I, but walking nonetheless. While leaning on a wheeled plinth (high table) and assisted by four therapists.

Two scuttled along on stools beside him (helping move his feet and covering his knees in case they "blew," as he says); another pulled the plinth in front; and a fourth followed behind with a lower plinth to fall back on, just in case.

After about twenty steps he collapsed, fatigued. The rest in the room, many on their own far more difficult journeys, cheered and applauded. One man who couldn't use his hands gave him a standing ovation.

Later one of our therapists told us she had never imagined that he would be able to do that. Another confessed to us that when Rick first came here, she didn't expect him to progress at all. Ever.

Whenever people say things like that, I tell them about our great God, about the prayers rising from our tremendous circle of support. We realize that these letters have gathered momentum of their own. Perhaps some of you reading these words are complete strangers. That's a mystery to us, but we thank you for your interest. It's our prayer that as many as possible will take encouragement for their own difficult situations from what God is teaching us here.

Many of you are not strangers. And you've been faithful to pray all this long while. You've followed us all the way down the West Nile, from the evening the pirates first attacked, through the battles with pain, and into these shallower, quieter, much slower waters.

To you, we say this: How we both wish you all could have seen those shuffling, hesitant but forward steps. But even in your absence, we felt you there in that room. God, through your prayers, lifted Rick's legs and helped him keep his balance and focus. Did you sense that? Amanda did. When I told her the good news about her father by phone, she asked me what time he took those steps. I told her. And she said:

"Mom, this afternoon around that time, a picture came to me of Dad walking.

Love and prayers,
Kathleen and Rick

Sunday, November 11

Today we had a date, Rick and I, at the Mackenzie Art Gallery next door, where this afternoon the Regina Light Lyric Opera Company performed a musical revue called *Songs That Won the War*.

In a brisk wind, threatening winter, Anthony pushed Rick across the street and up the small hill to the gallery. He had to leave shortly after and asked me if I would be able to manage him on the way back.

"I'll just let him out the doors and give him a little push," I said. "He likes that sort of thing."

I still haven't forgiven him for the ramp.

Most people who actually see those in wheelchairs are nice to them. The problem is that most people don't see people in wheelchairs. The chairs' occupants are like children: below eye level and convenient to ignore.

In the gallery's theater, the usher directed us to the only convenient place for a wheelchair — in a line of chairs pushed up against the back wall. The rest of the crowd milled past us.

Only one other person with a disability entered the theater, a senior pushing a walker. He rolled his walker past us without once looking down — right over Rick's toes, already sensitive and painful.

I can't help it. I've been chuckling all evening at his response: Rick took great offence at that walker rolling over his toes.

"Why me?" he asked me several times. "I'm the only one in a wheelchair. Why'd he have to pick me?"

In this entire voyage down the Nile, the man has never once asked, "Why, me?" He's doggedly asked, rather, "How? How can God use this to bring glory to himself?"

Perhaps the senior with the walker served to let the why out.

LlllllllllllllllllllllllllllllllllllllllllllllllllIIIIIIIIIIIIIIIllllll ... total accident — and what comes of writing after eleven at night.

Monday, November 12

A collection of visitors descended on us this morning. None knew about the rest, but somewhere in the middle of it all, seven of us joined hands and prayed there in the concourse where we visited, separated from the pirate ship in the courtyard by only a thick pane of glass.

Craig, rolling by, joined us.

Larry, our district superintendent, and his wife, Audrey — frequent, welcome visitors — were among them. As Larry lifted each of us to Father, my heart soared with his prayer, this blessing of benediction, this joining of hands — women, men, young and older, black, white, able, and other-abled, strangers and friends, in the middle of a public thoroughfare.

We had no other reason for it except to acknowledge God this day, to express our joy at what he has done and is doing in and through the circumstances that brought us here.

Wednesday, November 14

God keeps reminding us we're here by his allowance, for a higher purpose than we may ever know.

Each morning, Rick and I meet with each other and God in the solarium at the far end of the concourse, surrounded, outside the glass, by snow-capped evergreens, busy sparrows, chickadees, even the occasional white rabbit. The atmosphere there tunes our hearts and lifts our spirits.

But this morning we met in the hostel instead. The solarium is growing cold — and we're getting too many interruptions. Craig, who has lately joined us there, sent me an e-mail. A long one (for him). I shudder to think how much time it took him to write it. He missed us, and wanted us to know.

Our contact with this young man has grown and deepened. We must listen hard to the Holy Spirit to discover what the days ahead hold for this relationship. We can't stay here forever and I long to leave him with something strong he can lean on when we're not here. To introduce him to our living, active God, who frees those in spiritual prisons, who promises strength for each day and hope for tomorrow.

Friday, November 16
E-mail Update

Family and Friends,

As you know, when the pirates of the West Nile invaded our little boat, Rick was a pastor of a small church.

But a far broader church encompasses that little one. The church that Jesus founded is never bound by walls and doors and windows. Its membership list includes Christ-followers of many stripes and tribes around our community, our province, our country, and our world. Most have never set a foot inside our local church.

Members of Christ's church have overwhelmed us with a tsunami of kindness. They have sent flowers and gifts to help and cheer us. Their children have painted pictures for his hospital room walls. Some of the church's members and friends, often at great inconvenience to themselves, have provided for and loved us in myriad ways. They've extended encouragement to bolster us, knitted prayer shawls to warm us, provided food to nourish us. They've written cards, e-mails, and letters to remind us of God's healing power. Made countless phone calls to tell us they haven't forgotten us, sat and cried with us, held our hands and prayed with us.

It has been members of Christ's universal church who have, even from within their own crises — suffering losses that make ours pale in comparison — reached out to encourage us. Who have taken their prayers to the next level and skipped meals to pray for us instead. Who have driven for hours and entire days, simply to visit us at this rehab centre where we live temporarily. Who have offered and provided rides downtown so I could run some necessary errands. And who have planned a fund-raising event so that others in our local community who wished to help us could do so.

This church includes Christ-followers we barely know, some we know not at all. Strangers who reached out in Jesus' name. Like the Yorkton hospital receptionist who sent her prayers in a card. The elderly couple who tucked a well-worn (and crucial for their own needs) five-dollar bill into an envelope and sent it our way. The farmer who carried God's beacon of hope to us on one of our worst days. The mere acquaintance who reached deeply into her own resources to share them with us, because she felt God nudge her that way.

Where would we be without the church? The Catholic teacher who led her entire class in prayer for Rick. The organic farmer who has, every morning since this all began, provided me with breakfasts of his newly developed sprouted whole grain cereal. Neighbours who have mowed our lawn, raked our leaves, cared for our cat. Medical personnel who have become God's hands extended, God's goodnight whisper and good-morning smile.

Could we have gotten through the longest, darkest nights without the family of God, which encompasses and strengthens our own small one? No. No. A thousand times no.

The people in God's church who impact others most are always this kind of people: the ones who, when faced with need, do the wee (and big!) things God prompts even when they'll barely be noticed. That's how a tsunami is made: one vibration at a time, one drop at a time — and the wave is trickling into the lives of others here at this rehab center.

Love from Wascana in West Nile,
Kathleen and Rick

SUNNY SIDE UP
November 21, 2007

Beauty in the Beast

Craig Fisher is a fellow patient here at the rehab centre, a graduate of Regina's Campbell Collegiate, a musician, entrepreneur, and somewhat of a techno-whiz. He has magnetic steel-blue eyes, a smile that ignites them, and a bellowing laugh. When he's not on his computer, Craig spends his time either in bed or motoring about in the concourse in his electric wheelchair. Raising the blood pressure of onlookers as he careens between the brick pillars — striking only the occasional obstacle.

Craig cannot walk, easily control his limbs, feed himself, or speak. He communicates clearly nonetheless. His right arm goes up to say yes, his left arm to say no. And he sends e-mails from his specially adapted computer, a Herculean effort, because his arms go on parties all by themselves.

But Craig's primary way of talking to others is through a laminated sheet of words spread on the table attached to his wheelchair. He points to the words one at a time.

"How are you today?" I asked him once.

Up came his arm. It thrashed around a bit while finding its target, then plunged table-ward, thumb first, landing directly on a single word:

"Happy."

I had a foster sister who died when she was four of the same disease Craig has. It's a beast.

"Cerebral palsy is a horrible disease, isn't it?" I said to him once.

Down came that thumb again. Two words this time:

"NOT MINE."

⌒

Our son, Anthony, visited us here last weekend. We introduced him to Craig. They have things in common, those two. Anthony's a guitarist, loves people, enjoys the computer, is a whiz with electronic sound equipment.

While here, he showed Craig how to use the newest piece of recording equipment Craig had purchased. Then they tried it out, Anthony on his guitar, Craig on his electronic keyboard.

Technology facilitates Craig's music. As his body churns like butter in his chair, each of his movements is monitored by sensors, which translate his moves into music — music the electric keyboard played alone, firing out riffs and chords, arpeggios, and cadences. Music unlike any you've heard before.

Anthony played along on his old blonde guitar, his fingers skittering over the frets like spiders newly hatched. Floating over the soundboard. Strumming, picking, plucking, pausing.

The Preacher and I watched, aware that we were in the presence of profound magic, witnessing the blessed release, however temporary, of a man in a confinement too horrible to have been conceived by humanity, seemingly too merciless to have been ordered by Divinity.

Before my eyes the bars vanished and I saw, simply, two young men. Strangers — different in so many ways — brought to this moment through circumstances only God could have arranged. Jamming. Loving it.

And somewhere below, in the abyss where no music sounds, I hear what I'm sure is the angry roar of fallen, thwarted nature. Sometimes there's beauty in the beast. And God expects us to honour it.

Friday, November 23

One of Craig's dreams came true today. He had told us he would like the Regina *Leader Post* to feature him and his music. You can help with that, the Holy Spirit nudged me. So last week I interviewed Craig, wrote an article, and submitted it. Today I found a note from the entertainment editor. They want to run the article.

When I told Craig, his eyes became animated, he bellowed, and up went that right hand. "I ... make ... history ..." he pointed on his board, jubilant.

Craig seems to think that only his remarkable music makes him worth anything at all.

"Craig, what you do is absolutely amazing," we've told him. "But you know what? God made you a human being, not a human doing. Who you are is more important than what you do. You can inspire people who are completely able — you inspire us! — simply because of your great attitude."

He always listens quietly.

"Not only that," we keep reminding him, "but if you suddenly couldn't make music or be an inspiration to anyone, God would love you no less. You are important because you are beautiful in God's eyes, no matter your state."

Sunday, November 25

Anthony has returned, bringing more provisions. Barley cooked in the crock-pot overnight, topped with soymilk, raspberries, and saskatoons; whole-wheat toast with cornmeal butter on the side. Tasted like heaven. Only one more weekend with our daddy-long-legged son. How we'll miss him.

We walked after breakfast, he and I. Left Rick visiting with Craig and walked fast through the snow and unfriendly wind, making a half-hour circle, partway along the lakefront. Ducks and geese congregated in a small bit of water not yet frozen. And off to the side stood one lone pelican, half tipped.

We stood there watching it, willing it, wishing for it to move.

"I think its feet have gotten frozen into the ice," one of us said.

What hope, then, for the bird halfway home? For the one who stopped merely to rest, and discovered his haven had become a prison? What good, wings, when sky is forbidden?

Lord, sometimes I feel like a pelican here. The Nile is stretching long, and this cove, this place of rest and healing, has snared our feet.

Our Father, who art in heaven, free all of us pelicans.

Wednesday, November 28

Rick graduated to a walker today in his morning therapy. I had gone to the store for a few fresh vegetables, trying to race a storm that was forecast for later today. I'm so sorry I missed his graduation.

SUNNY SIDE UP
November 28

Advent: Absolutely Amazing Abundance

A mosquito took him down last August, but they're doing a marvellous job of rebuilding the Preacher here at Wascana. And God, our primary therapist, is restoring his spirit along with his health.

"It's Friday. Fantastic, fabulous, fun-filled, frolicking Friday."

He probably greeted the physiotherapists that way this morning; he has an alliterative phrase for every day of the week. I think he's driving those therapists crazy. One found a thesaurus and answered with a long list of her own.

But I didn't accompany him to his session today, precisely because it's Friday. The day I race article deadlines. So I've retreated to my hostel room to write.

Instead, I find myself distracted by the view from my window.

Below me lies a square courtyard featuring a well-treed children's playground.

No children play there today. Only a dawdling breeze that ruffles the black flag over the pirate-ship play structure, then wraps it gently around its pole before moving on to a new toy.

Snow.

Several flakes — consummate perfection — cling to my window. Most have landed far below on the slatted benches, the picnic tables, the raised four-leaf-clover-shaped sandboxes, softening the harsh edges of late autumn's bleakness. Instead of a dreary canvas, the playground has become a charming black-and-white sketch.

Black, too, are the windows evenly spaced in the other three walls that border the square surrounding the playground. But only a few are plain black; the rest have windowpanes: two white crosses per window.

Above, Canada geese depart by the hundreds from their summer feeding grounds at nearby Wascana Lake. Their columns ripple like ribbons as they arrange themselves for their southward journey. I hear their urgent honks through the double panes of my window. In a sky as white as the snow beneath, their silhouettes are as black as the flag over the pirate ship.

The pigeons congregating on the roof vents across the courtyard have taken to the sky, too, for the moment. They rose suddenly, like children released at recess. In the middle of their smaller black silhouettes I noticed a white dove.

The Preacher and I have seen that dove before. It reminds us of the sweet presence that has spread its wings over our sojourn here. God's Holy Spirit — like the snow, the windowpanes, the dove — has altered our perspective. Through his presence, the hard edges of West Nile neurological disease have become not tragedy, but opportunity. Not something horrible, but something beautiful. Not disabling, but enabling.

In the midst of bleak, God has visited us with loveliness. With the realization that hope isn't something that merely hovers. That peace is more than a promise, strength more than a suggestion, and love more than a lullaby.

That's the message of Advent. Absolutely amazing abundance, available only through a relationship with Jesus Christ.

Saturday, December 1
E-mail Update

Hi, All,

Clinic was short and sweet this week. Everybody seemed happy. Nurses, doctor, patient, patient's wife. Many of Rick's objectives have been met:

Talking well. Sleeping well. Thinking clearly. Sitting up. Dressing self. Washing self. Toileting self — with help. Bathing self — with even more help. Pain manageable, with help. Walking in walker with therapists' assistance. Coming to a standing position ... a little more work yet, but we're close. Stairs, in the next few weeks.

Left arm: still largely uncooperative. (Well, one can live without a left arm, right?)

During the previous clinic, I asked them about Rick's toes. They hurt all the time, I said. And he won't let me put lotion on them. They're getting scaly.

Sharon, the floor supervisor, held back a grin. "Doctor, put it in this man's chart to pray for his toes," she said.

Dr. Yip began scribbling as laughter rippled around the circle.

But I believe some may have applied the prescription.

"Are your toes still hurting?" I asked Rick days later.

"Not as much," he said.

◠

In the clinic's circle this week, Errin, who presides over these gatherings, added a new goal: going home.

"I don't know why it wasn't already on here," she said, sounding genuinely puzzled.

I don't believe for a moment she was. I think she waited until now on purpose. I think she realizes we need the subtle reminder that this place (safe, secure) was never intended to become our permanent residence. That it's her job to kick us out of here as soon as we're good to go.

We've talked to other temporary rehab patients here about home going. Similar apprehension skitters under our hopeful conversations like a mouse at a dinner party. We know it's not supposed to be there, we don't want to admit it, but there you have it. So finally we discuss leaving this place, this unusually wrought fellowship of those similarly afflicted and our fellow caregivers. And how we feel about it.

All of our lives — pre-West Nile, pre-stroke, tumour, accident, Guillain-

Barre syndrome, pre-whatever brought us here — all of them were cluttered with things that now are either impossible, improbable, unimportant, or unsafe.

Real life now seems rife with puzzles. Jobs (and clothes) that don't fit anymore. Deadly sidewalk cracks and doorjambs. Stairs you can't climb. Wheelchair-unfriendly cars and homes. Stockings that require legs. Friends you love who never once contacted you, and strangers you barely knew who did so regularly. Meals you have to cook and beds you have to make. Loud noises. Bright lights. And, for those of us on West Nile, mosquitoes next summer.

Home. Home. The sweetness of that word is now veiled with multiple question marks, not the least of which is, for us, "Where is home, exactly?" We live in a parsonage; it's attached to the job of clergyman, an occupation yet cloaked in uncertainty.

⌒

"I'm practicing to be a Wal-Mart greeter," Rick told our son Anthony this week.

Anthony has delighted us with his presence several times in the past month, last week bringing some of his homemade bread and vegan lasagna. He knows me. I began this journey as a vegan, evolved into an opportunarian, then a flexitarian, and now that things are more stable have returned to my vegetable-based diet, to guard my own health.

He looked at his dad and said with a dry chuckle, "Hey, that's no way to talk."

We hope, we expect, we pray that Rick will return to the pulpit. This week, for the first time, he asked that his large-print Bible be brought from home. During our six-pack reading — the usual five chapters from Psalms and one from Proverbs — he has begun to interrupt me to insert a few of his keen insights, hints of the return of my favourite pastor and Bible teacher.

In the end, where is home? For both of us, it has always meant going wherever God sends us. British Columbia. Manitoba. Ontario. Saskatchewan. Life as a Christ-follower is meant to be one of pilgrimage, which our present dwelling has taught us most of all. Home, ultimately, is nowhere here on earth.

Love,
Kathleen and Rick

Saturday, December 1
1 p.m.

Anthony arrived about ten last evening for his last visit before returning to his B.C. home. My heart feels carved out inside. Farewelling my dearest ones has always done this physical thing to me — like every other mother, I suppose.

After he left this morning, Rick and I sat in on the usual Saturday-morning mandolin orchestra rehearsal. They're playing Christmas music now, preparing for upcoming concerts.

Why did tears come today? There I sat, with the love of my life, crying at the glorias. I've cried so little on this pilgrimage. I don't understand myself at all.

SUNNY SIDE UP
December 5

By the Waters of Babylon the Nile

The Preacher's roommate fell on his way to the washroom one night recently. He wasn't badly hurt, thank God, but his bed shook, Rick said, and for the rest of the night their room was a hive of activity.

The combination of that mishap and an exhausting day following resulted in a lack of sleep that tuckered Rick out.

Two weeks later, he's still tired. We both are. I haven't felt like sitting down and having a good bawl very often on this trip, but tonight I do. (Don't feel sorry for me, please. By the time you send a note to say you are, my lifeboat will have righted itself. It always does.)

How wise of God to not show us ahead of time the bends in our rivers. I never dreamed the West Nile pirates would keep us in exile so very long.

When we came, trees still wore leaves. They're naked now. Snow covers the courtyards.

And they're decking the halls with boughs.

I can't even begin to imagine how the Preacher feels in his darkest moments, which — again, thank God — seem to be receding farther and farther into the backwaters of West Nile.

But tonight I have a better understanding of the captive Hebrews in Babylon, when their captors taunted them by requesting they sing. Psalm 137 recalls their answer:

By the rivers of Babylon we sat and wept ... How can we sing the songs of the LORD in this strange land?

We will celebrate Christmas. Right here at Wascana, with some of our new friends. And unlike the Hebrew captives, we will sing:

Emmanuel, Emmanuel ... His name is called ... Emmanuel. God with us ... revealed in us ...

Friday, December 7

Rick has had two roommates since arriving here. A third just moved in. A new comrade in arms. In fact, arms are the only limbs he has left. Irwin was both driver and victim in a bizarre hit and run incident a few months ago.

He arrived perplexed, wearing loss like a garment. It dragged down the corners of his smile. It seeped through every line in his wind-weathered, sun-beaten face. A face shaped by years of range-riding and ranch-tending. His own ranch, and very large.

The truck he drove was his farm truck, and it lost its brakes going down a hill. He either bailed or was thrown out, he can't remember, but the truck carried on without stopping — after running over him.

Friday, December 7
E-mail Update

Family and Friends,

Last week I told you that Rick has been re-learning to walk. This week he fell. Right on his "marvelous, magnificent Monday."

He had seemed to be doing well as his walker rolled and scraped across the polished floor. The therapists on each side had just finished congratulating him on his good form, careful steps, and upright posture.

Walking backwards in front of him, meeting his eyes to encourage him, I turned my head to glance quickly at something on the other side of the room. When I brought my eyes back, he wasn't there anymore.

He had gone down with no warning. Folded up like an accordion. Errin, ever vigilant, had stuck her knee under him as he fell, and there he squatted, looking up at me, one knee on the ground, one foot folded almost in half, his hands still clutching the top of his walker.

That happens rarely in that room, they told us. Ordinarily therapists can gauge when a person is safe to walk without collapsing. Rick's knees had been behaving nicely for several days. They still don't know what happened.

No one panicked, no one spoke. But other therapists, always on alert to what's happening elsewhere in the large room, scurried forward to help. Together they hauled him back up and into his chair.

"Good thing I've lost all those pounds," he said later.

He did injure that weak left arm again when he had left it up on the walker, but not significantly. An X-ray the next day indicated nothing broken, so only muscles and ligaments seem to have been affected, which will simply slow an already slow recovery.

Other than that, he had a good week. He's napping more often, though. One of the ongoing effects of this disease, we've learned, is chronic tiredness.

We have been surprised by the severity of West Nile neurological disease, and the lack of information out there about symptoms and possibilities. Since Rick fell ill, I've been contacted by others fighting these same pirates, many enduring far worse conditions.

The public deserves to have more awareness of West Nile, we think. We've been doing some research and (in case you hadn't noticed) this minor member of the media isn't shy to discuss it. We'd appreciate your prayers for wisdom and accuracy.

Back in Yorkton last night, friends and members of our community held a benefit dinner and auction for us. I didn't attend. Honestly, I think I would have melted in a puddle of tears if I had. Truly, we can't quite figure this out. As Rick told those gathered last night (by speaker phone), "We don't feel we're special. We're just ordinary people. God is taking care of us."

He is, indeed, through your kind hearts and open hands. I can't explain how overwhelmed we are, nor how profoundly grateful we are that God should arrange this way of helping provide for our needs.

Till next time,
Kathleen and Rick

Saturday, December 15
E-mail Update

To All Our Loved Ones,

Today I overheard a family member of a newly admitted patient say, "We're cancelling Christmas this year. There just won't be any."

I understood.

Popular culture, for those who enter the doors to these healing halls with suddenly broken bodies, slips away like an old snakeskin. It has no voice here. Like the rest of the three hundred people who make this their home, they're now prisoners in their own cells — some temporary, some permanent.

For a time at least, what the rest of the world is doing — even what we did in our former lives — becomes immaterial. So, despite gaily decorated trees, stockings on nurses' stations, and pine boughs on brick walls, Christmas — or Christmas as much of North American society commonly understands it — is lost, too.

Perhaps I also understood it wrongly. We've never made a splash of Christmas, our family, but what is Christmas without my favourite crèche? Three Christmas banquets? Rick's marvellous mashed potatoes? Pine boughs draped over our own fireplace? The waifs and strays (as we jokingly refer to the widows and wanderers we have long invited to join us) around our table? The pets tussling merrily in our discarded wrapping paper?

I've believed for years that Christmas must be more than all that. Perhaps, in the end, it isn't more. Perhaps it is less — far less. And very different.

Our exile here, courtesy of the pirates of West Nile, has required us to don different eyes — different hearts. Surrendering this time to God, for both Rick and me, has allowed us to view life — present and former — from a much different perspective.

And this year, in these healing halls, I've found a new understanding of Christmas.

Cliff walked his chair into our room and pulled up near me yesterday.

Rick had gone visiting Herb Restau, down the hall. Herb, who lost his leg to a Caterpillar while working on the oilfields, was admitted this week. Enjoying the quiet, I sat beside Rick's empty bed, my chair tipped back, tapping away at my laptop. I'm scheduled to teach several workshops (devotional-writing and journalling) in the New Year. Today was the day I had promised to get the promo material out to one of the groups' coordinators.

"You live on that thing, don't ya?" Cliff said, flashing me a broken-toothed smile.

I've grown tired of explaining my writing, so I fall back on the statement I've found satisfies curiosity best. "Some people knit. I write." It keeps the questions at bay.

When we first arrived here, Cliff reminded me of the mental image that I've assigned to the pirates I speak of when I refer to Rick's West Nile disease: mouth missing several teeth; eyes small, fierce, black; complexion swarthy; arms multi-tattooed with symbols I hate.

Cliff's therapy time overlapped Rick's, and daily we watched him struggle to fight back from ... what? We couldn't guess what had landed him in his tall wheelchair, curled his hands into useless claws, and weakened his flaccid limbs to the point where no strength or coordination remained.

Cliff made me shiver.

"I have a feeling that before he came here, this guy was pretty intimidating," Rick said one day after leaving physiotherapy. "We probably wouldn't have wanted to know him."

He's not intimidating now. Whatever brought him down did a thorough job of it. He could barely raise his head.

But Rick — post-Thanksgiving's marvelous answers to prayer — began to work at knowing Cliff. He started by simply saying, "Hi, Cliff," every time we passed him.

The man didn't answer at first, just stared. One day he grunted, and finally the grunt became a reluctant, "Hi." As his body grew stronger, his mind did, too, and after a month or so of Rick's continuous cheering him on in therapy, he began to reciprocate.

One evening, as I rolled Rick through the halls of our new neighbourhood, we saw Cliff sitting alone in his room.

"Take me in there," Rick said.

Honestly, I didn't want to. But Cliff had already seen us, so in we went.

Cliff turned his head from watching the provincial election coverage on his television, looked at Rick, and said, "Did ya watch the debate? I don't trust that guy." He tilted his head at one of the candidates.

The two men talked politics for a while, Cliff in his raspy, still recovering voice; Rick in his soft, also still recovering voice. Cliff's understanding of what he watched amazed me. I had never dreamt the man could have any brains left inside that battered body, and chastised myself for my assumptions.

Cliff didn't look at me, but he told Rick how he got in that chair.

"The way I got hurt ... I was drinking with some people and after I

drank with them they took me to my house ... and I don't remember ...
they beat me up there and left me there to die. My little niece found me
a couple days later. They're in the courts now, I think."

In our former life Cliff would likely have had nothing to do with Rick
either. Rick's white; he's not. Rick is a clergyman; I would hazard a guess
that wouldn't be acceptable to Cliff. No bridges were in place to help
these two connect.

But Rick rolled into his room in a wheelchair, a sling of canvas and
steel and silver-spoked wheels. His disability so like Cliff's, forged a
bridge, and the two have been friends ever since.

As Cliff sat in our room with me yesterday, chatting and rocking his
chair gently with feet that may never walk unassisted again, Christmas
enveloped me. As simply and quietly as that. No gifts, no tree or wrap-
pings, no lights or carols ... nothing but a man broken by life talking
freely with someone from outside his world. Utterly unlike him. A
woman — and a white one at that. A healthy woman. A wealthy (from
his perspective, at least) woman.

But a woman who nevertheless entered his life by crossing a bridge
someone else had built. A man like him, who suffered like him.

⌒

I have never experienced Christmas before, not truly, not like this year. I
have never felt it in my gut, not only my head, the profound miracle of
that baby in the manger who became my suffering Saviour on the
cross. Jesus Christ, God's Son, robing himself in brokenness like ours —
on purpose, mind you — so he could roll into our world and become
the bridge we could each cross to reach God.

Cancel Christmas this year? That's not possible.

Love,
Kathleen and Rick

Sunday, December 16

We sang carols around the piano in the concourse this morning. Craig, Vera and Irwin, Don and Glenda. Rick sang. Rick sang. Rick sang! Truly sang. How good to hear his bass voice once more.

Craig sang, too. When I asked him his favourite carol, he pointed, "Away in a Manger."

I played, and with great bellows and enthusiastic motions, he sang.

The Holy Spirit joined us, too, and throughout this day I sensed him surrounding us in an unusually intimate way.

Rick and I attended church in the chapel this afternoon. The lady pastor began with, "It's the oldest story in the world ... the story of not being where you want to be."

She reminded us — was she talking just to me? — that all through the Bible the people of God were looking for a home, some place where they could settle, somewhere where things would be perfect.

Yes, I thought. Home. Uncertainty surrounds us regarding the future. Home, I must remember, has no address here on earth.

After church, while Rick and Don rested, Glenda and I bundled up and walked around Wascana Lake. Hoarfrost decorated the trees, iced the hard surface of old snow, and turned this place into Wascana Wonderland.

Thirty-nine years ago today, Glenda and Don stood in a frigid snow-covered cemetery and buried their boy. Today, in a winter of another era, we West Nile Wives talked about our hearts. We talked all the way around the lake, cold air stealing our breaths, beauty soothing our hearts.

When we reached the Legislative Building we visited the black statue of the queen on her horse, threw ourselves into the snow, and made snow angels. Right there in the queen's presence.

We arrived back at Wascana just as darkness fell. The men seemed genuinely glad we'd escaped and had a good time.

Tuesday, December 18

In afternoon therapy, Rick hurt his shoulder again. It happened when Maggie asked him to roll on his tummy. He spent several moments with his head down on the mattress, while she leaned over him with the expression of a concerned Madonna.

These girls, Maggie and Errin, have been our daily hope, in forty-five-minute installments. We'll miss them sorely when we leave here. Just perhaps, they'll miss us, too.

Wednesday, December 19

Don and Glenda will go home for Christmas. Home. Where's that for us?

Rick feels he will be strong enough to resume ministry within a few months of returning, whenever that will be. But if we do return to the parsonage, and he doesn't get well, we'll have to leave to make room for the next pastor who, doubtless, will not be disabled.

The city rents a small wheelchair-accessible home, and they have offered it to us. But if we move into the little house, and he does get well enough to work, we'll have to leave there, too, to make room for someone who is disabled, because that little house is only for those who really need it.

It's almost comical. Somebody send in the clowns.

Friday, December 21
E-mail Update

Hi, Loved Ones All ... and New Friends, Too,

I decorated my room for Christmas: picked a few pine and spruce twigs on yesterday's walk around the lake, and came home and arranged them on my room's window sill, along with three mandarin oranges and a tiny pewter sparrow. The boughs for fragrance, the oranges for colour, and the bird to remind me that Jesus keeps me in his sights, even here in West Nile.

Christmas has begun to flow past us in an unusual way this year. Three times this week I was conscripted to play Christmas carols at various pianos around the complex for fellow patients both in rehab and in long-term care.

Up in the dining hall, these times feel like an after-dinner party, with friends sitting around calling out favourite carols. Yesterday, there were, let me see, Rick and Don, both suffering from West Nile; Rick's roommate, Irwin, a recent double leg amputee; Herb, a fellow from down the hall, also a recent amputee from a construction accident.

Together with us wives and other family members, there were around a dozen of us, I think.

Here's the wonder that will forever remain my Christmas miracle on the Nile. Rick is *singing* again. His bass voice has returned, as clear and firm as ever. The first time I heard him, I became so ecstatic that even his flat notes on "I Wonder as I Wander" blessed me. And I didn't think once, not even once, of how he might wander: On foot? In a wheelchair? By Paratransit?

Almost everyone's fighting something here. Pirates aren't exclusive to West Nile. We hold each others' hands and pray sometimes.

I'm often reminded of a hot, cloistered cement hovel in India. Ten feet by twelve, perhaps. Gathered there, one unexpected day, were many blind people. Ten? Twenty? Where did they all come from? I don't know now, and I didn't then. But I was there, too.

All I know for sure is that they surrounded my travel partner, Eldonna, and me, thicker than the flies that stuck to the walls, threatened our moist lips, and crawled on the soles of our bare sweaty feet.

They looked to us for help, but we had nothing to give them — nothing, that is, except the reassurance that Jesus Christ cared about them, and that if he didn't heal them then he would give them an even greater miracle: He would accompany them in their darknesses until the break of dawn.

But all they really wanted, they told us, was a place where they could live together and help each other. A place like these healing halls, perhaps. But in that part of India they would be lucky to get a set of concrete boxes joined together in a single line. Eldonna and I prayed for hope for them, and for strength.

Yesterday was the hostel's Christmas potluck. I brought a tray of veggies I had cut up, and Glenda brought fruit. The two of us ate circumspectly during the main course, but at dessert we turned into street urchins at a prince's feast.

Glenda is as disciplined an eater as I am, but neither of us knew ourselves. We shunned the healthy stuff, went straight to the home-baked sweets, and stuffed our faces. Then we laughed ourselves sick in amazement at our unfamiliar behaviour and did penance by taking a stiff walk for a good distance beside the lake, in the direction of the university.

I suppose we hostel-creepers are growing tired of not having our own kitchens to bake in, our own dainties to sample. We heat easy food — tinned goods, noodles, baked vegetables — in the microwaves at the hostel or nursing station, or eat in the cafeteria.

It all tastes the same now. But those treats tasted like home.

The friends we've made here are nearly all going home for Christmas. Rick and I are so excited for them, especially those who haven't been home since their accidents. We'll miss them, but this will be a good chance for us to get together with some of those we haven't been able to spend much time with lately.

Love and Joy come to you,
Kathleen and Rick

Sunday, December 23
Dancing with Craig

The Beans and their parents spent the day with us. Craig hung around most of the day, too, and to my delight, the little ones showed him nothing but kindness. I've explained often to Benjamin on other visits that Craig's body is broken — that it doesn't work like his does.

It's taken a few visits for the children to get used to Craig, but today Benjamin stood by his chair, touched his hand, and tried to talk to him. Craig reached out and stroked his hair, so very gently. We ate supper in the cafeteria. Craig joined us at the end. At the close of the meal, he asked if he could hold Tabatha. She seemed happy, so I plopped her on his chair table, intending to hold her there for just a few moments.

But as Craig's palsied arm encircled her like an iron band, Tabatha cringed, squealed, and reached for me, hanging onto me for dear life, whimpering.

I tried to remove her, but Craig's arm tightened. At the same time his chair started moving forward and began turning.

"He's taking off with my grandbaby!" I thought as I tugged and followed the chair.

But Craig didn't let go. The chair kept turning, scraping me on the shins and rolling over Amanda's foot as she also stood, shocked.

Craig bellowed. I pulled. Tabatha hollered. Amanda grabbed. The chair revolved. This went on for several rotations. Craig, it seemed, had gone mad, and was determined to make his break with my littlest Bean.

I fought harder to take her from him, trying to keep her from falling, from fear, and instead it was I who fell. Forward onto Craig's wheelchair table, still holding Tabatha.

Amanda, on the other side of the table, followed us around the merry-go-chase, as close to Craig's chair and Tabatha as her eight-month-pregnant tummy would allow.

Then I realized the problem. Somehow, as I had tried to place Tabatha on the table, her right foot had slipped over the edge and gotten stuck on the wheelchair control Craig uses to drive his chair. She had pushed it as far clockwise as it could go, creating the same effect as someone operating a vehicle with the wheel cranked as far as it could go.

I don't know how many rotations we made before Tabatha fixed things herself. She took her foot off, everyone calmed down, and we took inventory.

Tabatha, a little shaken, but okay. Craig, about the same, and a little perplexed. And Amanda and me, sheepish, but relieved.

It must have been our relief that brought our laughter. While Craig sat, still looking bewildered, Amanda and I laughed so loud and long that heads turned toward us from all corners of the cafeteria.

Finally, after our last gasps, I wiped my eyes, explaining my thoughts to Craig. When I apologized for misjudging him, he pointed furiously to these letters on his word board: "funny."

That's grace.

Saturday, January 5
E-mail Update

Family and Friends,

Ah, Christmas with the pirates. Without the usual preamble — the garland of banquets and plays, concerts and entertainment — it glided past on silent runners of joy, leaving only beauty and little time to tire of it. Leaving me, for the first time I can recall as an adult, with this thought: I'm so sorry it's over.

On Christmas Eve, Rick and I arranged a small gathering at the far end of the cafeteria, by the Christmas tree positioned beside the windows overlooking one edge of Wascana Park. We sit there often, watching the white world and the pine trees and the cars winding around the lake. Occasionally a giant snowball on a pogo stick races past: a jackrabbit in a colossal hurry.

We had arranged this gathering cautiously, Rick and I. Prayed over it fervently, not knowing how his body and mind would handle a public meeting, determined to keep things ultra low key.

God had arranged carol sheets weeks earlier, more or less dumping them into our laps. We distributed them. Rick welcomed everyone. I played. We all sang. Rick spoke. I read. We all sang some more. In between, we all spoke out of turn. Laughed and joked, eyeing the tray of Christmas treats and drinks we had arranged for after.

Thirteen people gathered in chairs and wheelchairs around that mellow white piano on Christmas Eve. Others had joined us there for carols in the evenings prior. Split-second people, many of them, their lives devastated in the space of a heartbeat. Some, but not most, were joined by visiting family members.

Strokes, cancer, beatings, amputations, vehicle accidents, mosquito bites ... different circumstances had brought us there. But on Christmas Eve we all had one thing in common. We couldn't spend Christmas where we most wanted to: at home.

Together we were testaments to the oldest story in history: the story of not being where you want to be.

It was the most unusual gathering of people we've ever joined. People in the throes of major life upheaval. Souls ragged with questions, bodies ravaged by a multitude of monsters, madmen, pirates, and beasts. Some wondering whether God really cares. If he sees. If it matters anyway. Questioning the true meaning of Christmas.

Two nurses slipped in partway through, and our Regina friend, May, joined us, too.

Did you catch what I said earlier? Rick spoke. I wrote those words quickly, almost afraid to blink, in case my memory was deceiving me.

As evidence of the healing that God has thus far brought about, through his power and your prayers, Rick spoke. For a good ten minutes.

First he rolled his chair over to Cliff. Then he put his hand on his arm and told the story of God sending Christ to Planet Earth. Disabled by humanity, robed in rags, destined for unspeakable suffering. Jesus, who became, on the cross, the bridge between us and God.

In a similar way, Rick said, his own disablement, though temporary, helped build a bridge between himself and Cliff. And made possible a friendship that previously would never have been possible.

Rick said all that, without a stutter, without a falter.

And so it came to pass that on our first Christmas Eve after the pirates' invasion, we rejoiced at what God has done. That he sent his Son. That he's bringing healing to these broken bodies. That he offers hope to all our sin-broken spirits.

In spite of the pirates,
Kathleen and Rick

Wednesday, January 2
At Cliff's Edge

It came to me as I placed a forkful of carrot cake in Cliff's mouth, past his scarred brown skin and cracked lips: I love this battered Indian, this scrap of invalid humanity with bad tattoos and a mouth like a piano missing half its ivories. This man with the grasshopper voice.

One day I asked him, "Cliff, was your voice like that before your beating?"

"Yep. When I was thirteen I got a rope and put it around my neck and tried to hang myself. That's why it's like that."

So said this man who has escaped hell numerous times, surviving a violent childhood, residential schooling, a suicide attempt, numerous beatings. This man whom God and the pirates have arranged for us to meet.

I'm astonished by this love. I have no excuse for it. Cliff has nothing to offer. He won't be in my life for long. He visits me, as I sit in Rick's room writing, only because I'm attached to Rick, whom he admires. But I want to protect him. I don't want to see him hurt any further. And I'm worried about his future, about the wide variety of hells he still has before him. I wish I could snatch him out.

Cliff entered this New Year in a foul mood. Arriving at therapy this morning, he was slumped in his chair, almost out of it.

"You should wear your seat belt, Cliff," Errin told him kindly. "You're going to fall out of there."

Rick and I told him the same thing yesterday. He had complained that he was slipping, so I hoisted him up, and Rick helped fasten his belt. But today he would have none of it from the therapists.

"I didn't come here to be lectured," he said. "I don't need a lecture."

He almost returned to his room, but changed his mind and walked his chair back in, parking close to Rick's therapy couch. I went over and sat and talked with him for a few minutes. I didn't mention the seat belt.

Later, back up on the ward, he rolled in to say hello, as he's been doing regularly. He wants to find out how Rick is feeling about his therapy, and as always he encourages him in his simple way.

But today he told us that he had been informed he would likely never walk again without a walker. He's taking that pretty hard. He had already been told he may never be capable of feeding himself again. And now this. No wonder the man has been sore.

I suddenly had an idea. Or rather, God gave me an idea.

"Cliff, I have a story for you."

And I told him the story of Joseph. There's a pack of details in that story, but I'm a big-picture person, and that's how I told it: Man has trouble. Man obeys God and keeps his integrity. God works it for good. The end.

But Cliff needed more than that. He comes from a storytelling tradition, so the more details I could put in, the better. I prayed as I went, "Lord, help me out here."

I got many of those details wrong. I could sense Rick behind me, looking out at his slice of sky above the brick wall opposite his window. Biting his tongue. I called Potiphar a king. I got the butcher and the baker mixed up, and jumbled up the dreams. Blessed man, he never once corrected me.

But I got one thing right: I told Cliff what Joseph told his brothers, in the end. "You meant it for evil, but God meant it for good."

"Cliff," I told him, "God has a bigger perspective on your beating than we can see right now. One day you may look back and thank God for it. Can you think of anything good that has happened to you because of it, even now?"

He paused for a moment. "I met youse," he said, thrusting out his chin.

"And there will be more," I told him. "God wants you to meet Jesus, too. Those guys who beat you up meant to harm you — but God can change it into something good. Just watch."

Cliff nodded his grizzled head.

"Yep," he said, and walked his chair out of the room.

SUNNY SIDE UP
January 2, 2008

West Nile Wives Dancing

Before the pirates of West Nile attacked their little boat, Don and Glenda Bell sometimes danced together. They told the Preacher and me this one evening as we listened to a band here at the rehab center.

Only the long-term residents danced that night. It's the custom here. Staff, some bobbing in rhythm, pushed the patients' wheelchairs in figure eights around towering indoor fig trees. Some patients grinned. Others waved at the watching wallflowers.

West Nile disease robbed Don of his mobility and landed him here. Don's a farmer, full of fight and sinew. Their similar conditions have made him and the Preacher companions on this journey. Like brothers in different classes, they regularly compare notes after therapy sessions.

A few weeks ago, while relearning to walk, both men fell.

On Monday (his marvellous, magnificent Monday, as he alliterated that particular day of the week) the Preacher went down like a stone. Two days later, Don followed suit.

The battle to regain what the pirates stole takes jags that no one, even therapists, can predict. I call it the dance of West Nile. Three steps forward, two back. The forward steps are increasing, but when progress turns inside out, the only thing to do is thank God for the good steps previous, grab onto hope, and carry on.

Don has a private nurse — his wife, Glenda. I enjoy the company of this gracious lady with prematurely lace-white hair. Our futures loom with question marks, but we laugh often. And walk together — very fast. I've dubbed us the West Nile Wives.

When we thread ourselves through the rabbit warren of these healing halls, people get out of our way. The other day as I approached, a woman pasted herself to the wall like a postage stamp, panic in her eyes.

"I'm going to get T-shirts made," I joked one morning. "West Nile Wives Walking. Stand Clear."

Recently our grandbeans visited the Preacher and me while their parents shopped. Prematurely pooped after far too short a time, Rick rolled himself off to his room for a nap. The children and I wandered into the empty concourse where a pianist was playing ragtime.

Don and Glenda rolled up, too. The children bounced on the couch, Don tapped his toes, and I looked at that vast sheet of polished floor.

"Let's dance!"

Glenda joined us, her movements graceful and lively. I held Tabatha in my arms, twirling her inside Benjamin's larger circles, his streamlined little body racing fast.

There's a lot we can't do, here in West Nile at Wascana. A lot we may never do again, the Bells and us. But that afternoon the West Nile Wives, grabbing hope, did a dance of their own. For gratitude for life, for the moment's joy — perhaps for a better year in 2008.

And I believe the Lord of the Dance, the Divine Choreographer of all life, joined in.

SUNNY SIDE UP
January 9

The Gospel According to the Pirates

Our friend Ken Dressler, who is filling the Preacher's pulpit for now, called us here at the rehab centre the other evening. We had just begun our put-the-Preacher-to-bed routine. I fumbled for the phone anyway.

"Hello, Ken," I said. "Can I call you back in ten minutes or so? We're just starting our West Nile Pole Dance."

Ken paused. 'Uh ... okay."

I didn't understand why he paused. Later his wife, Sharon,

told us that he'd hung up and said, in a rather shocked tones, *"They're pole dancing now."*

Ah, those West Nile pirates. At their hands (and mine, Lord forgive me), our most private routines have become public property, our intimate conversations the coffee chat of strangers.

I had described that dance in an earlier e-mail, but our friend needed reminding (and perhaps wifely assurances) that his predecessor hadn't abandoned his high calling to undertake a more titillating vocation.

The West Nile Pole Dance is how we get the Preacher (who can't quite reach a standing position alone) onto the throne. Like the less wholesome version, it involves a steel pole. And a belt, and various stages of undress.

Maggie, his occupational therapist, taught us every step. In case the pirates attack you similarly, you should know at least the first part.

First, we enter the washroom. Close the door behind us. (Considering that you're reading this, I wonder why we bother.)

Inside, I place a plastic riser on the toilet seat, buckle a physiotherapy belt around the Preacher's still shrinking waist (he's lost dozens of pounds these last four months), and roll his chair up to a johnny pole: a steel post in the floor beside the toilet. He reaches for it with his strong right arm.

I stand on the pole's opposite side, also holding it with one hand, and grab his therapy belt with the other. Then I lower myself to a semi-crouching position and place my knees directly on his.

"And-a-one, and-a-two, and-a-three," we count aloud. On three I push his knees and pull on the belt. Our combined strength enables him to pull himself up on the pole. Holding on, he steps around it to the toilet, carefully. He blows a knee occasionally.

The remaining steps I leave to your imagination.

Each evening, I contribute less strength to our West Nile Pole Dance. The Preacher gets stronger daily. He hopes to be independently toilet trained before our grandson.

Friday, January 11

Larry and Audrey visited this afternoon, in the double capacity of friends and district superintendent. We're still trying to thrash out the housing issues, to no one's satisfaction. There are far too many what-ifs, the answers to which depend on Rick's future health, and only God knows that. Living in a parsonage, though I've loved it, complicates this situation for everyone, us and the church.

The other complicating factor is Rick's future work at the church. "How do you want to try to make the re-entry, if you feel well enough to try to return to work?" Larry asked.

Rick hadn't thought about that.

Then he asked something else, something unexpected.

"And how do you want the church to tell you if they feel they'd like a change of pastor?"

"Put a red flag at our front door?" I suggested, remembering the pirates.

We all chuckled, but we didn't come up with an answer.

Saturday, January 12
E-mail Update
The Pied Piper of Wascana

Rick has taken to playing a five-dollar recorder I recently bought at a booth selling handmade items from Peru. I gave it to him at Christmas. It's a lovely thing, hand-carved from a hollow stick, lacquered to a fine black gloss, with geometric and floral designs etched all round.

He coaxes a sweet tone from that black recorder, one that rivals a mellow flute, but with slightly deflated notes. The pirates of West Nile robbed a little more of his already slightly diminished hearing, but we can't blame the pirates for those flat notes. Truth is, he's always had a bit of a tin ear.

Maggie, his occupational therapist, loves the recorder. She encourages him to use it as much as possible. "It'll increase your left hand dexterity," she told him. (Maggie has also put his *right* arm in a sling:

constraint therapy, she calls it, a way to encourage the limp left one to work harder.)

I call him the Pied Piper of Rehab these days. He serenades people, wherever he parks his wheelchair. He plays "Jesus Loves Me," "Amazing Grace," "The Way That He Loves," and "Our Great Saviour." His repertoire is limited. When he runs out, he plays the theme from the old kids show *The Friendly Giant.*

I'm not the only one who thinks of him as the Pied Piper. On New Year's Day, as he sat playing just inside the front doors, a man walked in, laughed, looked around as though searching for something, and said, "Hey ... where are all the mice?"

Each evening close to bedtime, Rick rolls down the hall to Chantelle's room and plays her goodnight.

Picture a weathered crabapple tree, its trunk gnarled and twisted. Picture a bulge on that twisted trunk about the size of a child's head. Picture two branches coming from just below that, bending downward and clinging to the trunk, and at their extremities bent up again, tightly, with tiny folded up hands at the end of each.

Cut off that twisted trunk above the bulge. Chop it off again just below it, at about the length of a four year old. Split the bottom vertically into two, following the twists so they're separate, but not really. Add something that resembles feet at the bottom.

Now put human skin on the trunk instead of bark and hair and eyes on the head-sized bulge: short mink hair that sticks straight up, and eyes that show more white than colour.

Now give that picture a voice. The heart-rending cry of an abandoned kitten.

You have just drawn Chantelle. She shares the ward with us.

A cerebral palsy victim, Chantelle is about the length of a four-year old. She's here because her mom is ill and can't care for her just now.

Chantelle can't communicate, but her eyes follow anyone who'll stop to speak to her. When Rick comes to visit, they trace his every movement. He can't go in because she's in isolation, so he just sits in her door instead, playing.

That, and learning to use a computer again, is what Rick does now, for occupational therapy. He plays for people. And to this little one who has no voice, no choice, and no mother, for a time.

He talks to her first, speaking softly, as though she was a normal twenty-two year old. He uses big words and no baby talk.

"Hi, Chantelle. It's Rick again, coming to serenade you on my recorder. I had a totally terrific tremendous Tuesday today. How about you?" The woman-child politely stops her cries. Listens. He plays then. All the songs in his repertoire.

Chantelle's feet can't follow the Pied Piper of Wascana when he leaves her doorway. But her eyes do, all the way past the doorjamb. Sometimes she cries. Sometimes, then, an understanding nurse dons isolation garb, picks her up and cuddles her. But sometimes she seems almost to smile, ready to sleep.

In Christ,
Kathleen and Rick

Sunday, January 13

Craig, given his circumstances, has rarely had the opportunity to think of others. But I told him about Chantelle and their common disease, and one afternoon he came onto our ward to see her. The meeting, if you could call it that, has changed him.

When Craig learned how much Chantelle enjoys Rick's music, he suggested that he make a CD for her. A CD of his own music, we imagined he meant. He wanted Rick to help him.

When Rick arrived in his room, Craig explained his true intent: He wished to make a CD of Rick playing the recorder, to play for Chantelle when Rick can't enchant her anymore with his music.

⟶

After lunch, Rick lay down to sleep. I drew the curtain, sat beside him with computer on lap. Suddenly ...

"Rick!"

Rick turned instantly in the bed. Lifted his head. "Yes, Cliff?"

"Whatcha doin' behind there?"

"Resting."

"It's too damn early to rest."

With that Cliff rolled his chair into our room, right past the curtain. And that's life on the wards.

Wednesday, January 16

Rick and I read from a small devotional book, *Our Daily Bread*, each night, along with roommate Irwin. As we prepared to do so tonight, I asked, "Is anyone else here cold?"

"Not me, I'm hot," Rick said.

"No, I'm okay," Irwin said. "Just my feet are a little cold."

I almost offered him a blanket before I remembered that Irwin has no feet.

Both men chuckled.

"Took her a good thirty seconds," Rick said.

I always rub lotion on Rick's feet at night, but I had his feet tucked in before I remembered. "Do you want me to rub your feet?" I asked him, preparing to un-tuck.

"I'm okay," he said.

Just because those two guys had given me a hard time for being so slow a few minutes earlier, I asked Irwin, "Do ya want your feet rubbed?"

"Sure," he fired back. "Do you have them over there?"

We're doing other things together, too. As we've plied the waters of the Nile, I've done almost all the oral praying. Tonight I insisted Rick pray the evening prayer. It's only fair — every night I read the scripture, Irwin reads the book, and I pray. Rick just sits.

"It's time," I told him. I could see the panic in his eyes, but I didn't budge. Finally, he bowed his head and prayed. He wasn't talking to me, but I overheard anyway, and the words that emerged carried a new firmness, a beautiful softness.

"There, now. That wasn't too hard, was it?" I said.

I explained to Irwin that Rick's encephalitis initially scattered his thoughts all over the map, and that he still doesn't trust his ability to string a spontaneous prayer together in the presence of others.

"You didn't do half bad," Irwin said to Rick.

Irwin knows about prayer. He told us of his family members — among them a missionary and a pastor — who are praying for him.

Saturday, January 19
E-mail Update

Hi, Family and Friends,

Both Rick and May have been chiding me over my lack of eating and sleeping.

"You must sleep," May told me. "We worship God with our bodies. Sleep is one way to worship."

"No," I argued. "Sleep is passive. Worship can't be passive. It's intentional. A gift. Something we offer God to honour who he is, and it must cost us something. Sleep isn't worship."

But perhaps she's right about the need for more shuteye. At least six people have told me in the last few days that I'm looking tired. I'm not neglecting myself in the least. But when I leave Rick at night, I have a long stretch of hours I know won't be interrupted by anyone or anything. I write best in that state. It's not a luxury; it's mandatory. And it's hard work. It's my form of worship.

During May's last visit, Don and Glenda joined us in the hostel kitchen. Glenda cut up an apple and offered it to us all. A huge apple, gold, blushing red. John-a-gold, read the sticker. May refused; she hadn't had supper yet.

I stuck the plate in her face. "Eat, May. It's a form of worship."

She ate.

I'll soon be able to get more sleep, perhaps. The shore is clearly visible on the banks of the Nile now. Rick has made phenomenal progress just since Christmas. This past week Errin and he began working on one of the final holdouts, actual stairs. He's also mastered transferring himself into and out of a car. And in his therapy session yesterday he managed to get himself up from the floor onto a small stool.

As a caregiver, there's one thing I didn't anticipate — becoming unnecessary.

Rick doesn't need me anymore at the johnny pole. Now, when Rick gets up from his wheelchair in the washroom, using only the steel pole for support, I supervise him instead. Stand opposite him as before, but helping only if needed. Willing my body to remain straight, my knees to stay clear of his. To refuse providing that extra push that makes his rising so much easier.

I'm going to need help letting go of my role as Rick's caregiver when we leave here.

When we leave here. Joy should accompany that thought. Instead, I find the question marks regarding our future looming ever larger. It's the discomfort of transition, I know, but also (for me, at least) the groping to understand what God would have us now do with all he has shown to us, done for us, been to us, made of us in these past months.

As we grope for a new vision of life and ministry — one that God has already been providing here, among these broken people — I am comforted by the thought that God knows all our roads, behind and before. He will not abandon us now.

I am also challenged by this thought: I refuse to leave this place and time unchanged. Like our mosaics, I will be re-assembled. Softened. Hardened. Tempered. New. And still grateful for ...

Strength for today, hope for tomorrow.
Kathleen and Rick

Tuesday, January 22

Rumours have floated, like debris on the currents of the Nile, that despite God's miraculous work in Rick's body, the church board has decided to search for a new, able-bodied pastor.

Of course it is their perfect right to do so, but I don't believe it. Surely the people Rick has loved and served and taught and laughed with for almost two decades will welcome him back, will wait a few more months for his strength to return, will be eager to see what God has done in the life of their long-time shepherd, will embrace him in his weakness. It's what Jesus would do, church policies aside.

I sat on the bed last night after I got into my room. Wanting to cry, knowing I should cry, but unable to cry. Wishing for someone, anyone, to hug me and tell me everything will be okay at the end of the Nile. Then I got into bed and tried to sleep, tried to pray, tried to see Jesus' face until around four this morning. I did sleep finally, then woke and read the Psalms, prayed, got up, had devotions with Rick.

⌒

I heard the wails tonight. They advanced down Wascana's halls like a full-blown funeral procession. Someone down there, I knew, was doing some serious shoulder heaving.

I followed that sound, pulled as if by magnets past the darkened rooms of already sleeping patients, past a nursing station, and around the corner into a ward I had often visited. The sobs increased in volume as I neared Bonny's room. In fact, they were coming from her room.

I've met Bonny (not her real name) just a few times. Though in her mid-forties, she is a woman-child. She has Down's syndrome, and lives here at Wascana. She goes to a sheltered workshop during the weekdays.

Because I've only ever walked by her room in the evening, I've only ever seen her sitting on her bed in her flannel nightgown, rocking to and fro, waiting for bedtime. Sometimes she watches a television placed just a few feet in front of her weak eyes.

I've gone in and spoken to her a few times. She always responds with effusive cheer.

Not tonight. As usual, Bonny was sitting on the edge of her bed in her darkened room. But instead of staring at the television or into the lighted hall, she sat hunched over, her hands in her face, as she turned her heart inside out.

Her sobs came from such a deep place I knew that no words would help. It would be like placing a towel on the beach to sop up a tsunami.

So I plopped down beside her on the bed, and placed an arm around her shoulders. And said nothing.

"I have a sore tummy. I miss my mommy," she said, turning her whole body toward me, flinging both arms around me and tucking her head under my chin. My nostrils filled with the fragrance of her coconut-scented, freshly washed hair.

She had a sore tummy. I had a sore heart. Both our little boats had entered rough waters. As our safe harbours faded into the mists of uncertainty, we each mourned the loss of the comfortable familiar.

A robust hug doesn't fix those things, but it helps. Even this simple woman knew that.

"Bonny, I think God sent me to give you a hug tonight. Or maybe he sent you to give me a hug!"

She nodded and held onto me more tightly.

After we'd hugged three or four minutes, her tears falling on my sweater and mine on the arm of her flannel nightgown, her sobs dwindled to spasmodic hiccups. Her shoulders barely heaved now, but we stayed locked in that hug for several more minutes.

Two nurses came in, sat down beside us, watched and left without speaking to me.

There wasn't much to say, really. God was doing all the talking in that dark room. To this lonely, middle-aged writer, and that little red-eyed Down's syndrome woman, he spoke in silent eloquence of his vigilant love.

⌒

Rick is walking well now, still with a walker, but without a "follower" and with only one person walking beside. I watched him this morning go up and down the stairs with Errin at his side. After his walk, she had him attempt to get up off the floor — the mat, actually — and seat himself on a short stool. I watched him squirm around on that mat, trying to get into position to get up. It looked like break dancing — the geriatric version.

⌒

Today we met Jen coming in to therapy as we were leaving. After we chatted awhile I reached down to hug her. She hugged me back with as much strength as her paralyzed arms would allow.

"Don't get enough of those in here," she said.

Thursday, January 24

Maggie has been preparing Rick for all that waits him at home. In the little "practice house" down in Occupational Therapy, she gave him his assignment: to get in and out of the bathtub, fully clothed. While she watched, arms folded, face thoughtful, he grabbed the grip bar with his right hand, stepped slowly and carefully over the side, sat on the edge, then managed a not-so-neat slide to the bottom.

"Well done!" she said.

Getting out was another story. He simply couldn't bring himself up and became quite stuck in the process.

I wondered if we'd have to bring in a lift, but Maggie and I managed alone, losing only one belt loop in the process.

I took photos of him sitting there, fully clothed in the bathtub, a bemused look on his face.

He weighs 213 pounds now. When he came into hospital in Yorkton, he weighed, if memory serves, 283 or thereabouts. Seventy pounds of fat and muscle. Gone.

"I'm only half the man I used to be," he says.

I'll take that half and love it.

Tuesday, January 29

In the hostel tonight, Don and Glenda, Irwin and his wife, Vera, Herb Restau and his wife, Carol, Rick and I, and a few other friends sat around one of the dining tables swapping stories. The fellowship of the similarly afflicted, I call us. While we kicked around our shared hospital experiences, Rick made a slight complaint about my telling him when he has to go to bed.

Sometimes on the ward at night, when I'm dog tired (which often happens around eight or eight thirty, before I get my second wind and sit to write for hours, Rick decides he wants to go visiting other patients in their rooms. People who count on him. Chantelle, to whom he plays his recorder, Cliff, and others.

I follow, smiling and chatting through my weariness, until finally I realize I'm going to fall down, so tell him abruptly that it's time for him to go to bed.

"From now on then, you can put yourself to bed," I said, when he made that little peep of complaint. (He really doesn't make a practice of that.) "You're a man. If you can stand up to pee, you can put yourself to bed."

The other patients, having faced this same dilemma themselves, roared with laughter.

But I'd forgotten that the curtain between the ward beds isn't soundproof. Irwin, who may be missing two legs, but has exceptional ears, told the others of a conversation he heard between us shortly before.

"He told her the other night that he feels like a real man now that he can stand up to pee," he said with a big grin. "She told him, 'Even little boys stand up to pee. That doesn't make you a man — you've got something else to do before you can call yourself a man."

The others' laughter drowned my protests, but couldn't hide my crimson face.

Thursday, January 30

We attended clinic this afternoon and discussed a date for going home. One by one, Errin went through the goals for Rick, until we all realized that almost all been reached. Last question, posed by Dr. Yip: "Is this person safe to go back into the community?"

Long pause. Then both physiotherapists said yes, and Tracie the social worker nodded in agreement.

The team has suggested we take a weekend pass and travel to Yorkton to test whether or not Rick can handle the parsonage stairs. We'll book a bed in respite care at the nursing home and try the stairs on an afternoon visit home.

We'll also attend our own beloved church, and Rick will greet the people he's led for almost seventeen years, letting them see what God has done through the prayers of his people.

Glenda and I walked tonight, briskly through the basement and every floor. How I'll miss these times, this lady, this place, this front-row seat in the theatre where God's healing power blooms.

Saturday, February 2
E-mail Update

Family and Friends,

We're on the home stretch, we hope.

"Everybody's goin' their own way," Cliff said, when he walked his chair into Rick's room the other day. "Why does everybody have to go their own way?"

He knows we'll be moving on soon.

When we returned from Yorkton last weekend, he ran us through a grand inquisition. Had our trip gone well? Yes. Had Rick been able to climb the stairs into the parsonage? Yes, with just one almost-tumble on the second time in, saved by my knee.

Did he preach? Yes ... unintentionally.

"I just told some of our stories, some of the things God has done here in the last few months," Rick told him.

He told those stories standing out of his wheelchair, leaning occasionally on a pew, and did so for twenty minutes.

I'm a little biased, so forgive me. I've watched this standing miracle unfold, and I wanted to rise, to shout for joy, to applaud for God. I remained sitting, quietly, in my usual spot, second row, piano side, listening to the sniffles behind me. How I wished our congregation could have all seen the things I've seen, the way God has been at work re-creating, even as recently as the last few weeks.

After he finished grilling Rick, Cliff looked at me with a grin worthy of the most wicked pirate.

"Did you have a bath?"

There are few secrets here among the patients and family who live on the inside. Cliff knows (thanks to Rick) that I've only had one bath in almost five months; there's only a shower in my hostel room.

Sometimes on Friday nights, while bathing my patient husband, I've wanted to crawl right into that deep tub with him.

But last weekend I had my bath at the parsonage, in the ivy-stencilled bathroom with the yellow walls, with Moses the cat keeping watch. It's been a while since he's had company in the house, after all.

We enjoyed a fabulous, busy weekend, and we celebrated what God has done. In spite of the pirates. We hugged our kids and played with the grandbeans (despite orders, that littlest bean hasn't yet arrived). Worshipped in our own church: a little like heaven, that. Visited with our beloved neighbours. Attended a musical. And finally arrived back at Wascana utterly exhausted. But it was a good tired.

Cliff lapped up every detail, seeking a taste of something that may not be his for a very long time, if ever.

In the absence of effective recovery from his beatings, he'll soon be transferred to the other side of this rehab centre. The long-term care side, where Craig lives. I worry about our warrior friend.

"Cliff, know what? If I could, I would take you home with us and take care of you."

"Yeah, right," Cliff said.

He says that often.

Every time he catches me pecking away at this computer, he asks me what I'm writing now.

"I'm writing a book about you, Cliff," I say, tongue in cheek.

"Yeah, right."

"Cliff, know what else?"

"What?"

"You know how Rick and I have Jesus for our friend? The Bible tells us that one day we'll go to heaven. Come with us. Over there, we won't have to go our own ways."

Rumours have flown concerning our future plans. You can say you read the truth here. We have always hoped and anticipated that when we leave here we'll return to the parsonage that's been our home for almost two decades.

But everyone involved recognizes the uncertainties revolving around Rick's health. They also realize that the house we've called home doesn't belong to us. It belongs to a church that very much needs a permanent pastor able to shepherd its people and oversee its future direction.

If, for whatever reason, Rick cannot soon resume ministry, God has graciously provided an option for our time of transition. In view of soaring local housing costs, we've been offered the possibility of renting a lovely barrier-free-access house for as long as Rick needs it.

We've not committed ourselves, and won't know more until the middle of February, but last weekend we toured the house.

It's much smaller than the parsonage. It would take a peck of weeding our stuff. But I could be happy there, I realized, as we toured that little house. A reaction that surprised me, because making peace with that possibility hasn't come easily for me. But over the years, God has taught me how to bring myself into a neutral position when faced with potential change or difficult decisions.

Our future home, whether the parsonage at 87 Mossfield Place or elsewhere, will fill up at times with family and friends, with laughter and song, and the hospitable spirit of Christ. Because we choose it to. That much we know, and in that I find serenity.

Meanwhile, we remain here in these healing halls for what may be only a matter of weeks, until Rick's team is able to help us obtain occupational therapy and physiotherapy back in Yorkton.

He's walking with the walker all over the ward now, wearing jeans and actual shoes. "Gee, you're tall," he gets regularly. He's only four foot four in his chair, but when he stands, his growth spurt to six foot one is a bit of a shock for the smaller nurses.

Love,
Kathleen and Rick

Monday, February 4

"Pray for that grandbean's safe arrival." I don't know how often those words replayed themselves in my head and heart last night. I've heard that soft whisper often enough, not in actual voice, but impressions, to know the Holy Spirit wanted to give me an assignment.

So I prayed, almost all night.

Amanda has had several nights of labour that didn't produce anything. But Kendall called in the middle of my prayers last night to announce that our latest grandbean had arrived safely.

Amanda called me from her hospital bed later. Euphoric. Dinah Jane was born at 3:58, after slightly less than two and a half hours of labour: eight pounds, twelve and a quarter ounces, twenty-one and a half inches long.

"Mom," she said, "did Kendall tell you she has lots and lots of curly blonde hair?"

No, he hadn't. I want to go see that baby, my baby, all my Beans. I will, too. Pirates, please release me, let me go, for I don't love you anymore. My babies need me.

I rushed over to Rick's room early this morning to tell him the news, then left for a walk.

When he came to my hostel room for devotions, I noticed a piece of paper pinned to his chest. "It's a girl. Dinah Jane Buhler. 8 lbs. 12 and 1/4 oz," it proclaimed.

He wore it for the rest of the day.

Wednesday, February 6

The pirates have released me. It was cold today, thirty below or something. But with no snow predicted, I left Wascana and Rick earlier this afternoon and drove the two hours to Yorkton without stopping.

When I turned into the hospital parking lot there I spotted Kendall and the children walking toward the doors. When I honked, Kendall and Benjamin both turned. In the frightful cold, Kendall turned back toward the doors, but Benjamin stopped and stared at me for one long moment before his father took him into the warmth of the foyer.

I caught up with them inside. Tabatha kept staring as though confused by finding me there. Even Benjamin seemed a little shy. He didn't come to me as he usually does. I've been gone too long, I'm afraid.

In the hospital room, Amanda, wearing yellow pajamas, awaited us. As I hugged my own baby girl (how did she get to be a mother of three?), Tabatha pointed, "Baby in 'puter," she said. Dinah Jane Buhler lay sleeping spread-eagled in a clear plastic bassinet under ultraviolet lights to chase away her jaundice.

I almost drowned in her dark eyes, and loved her immediately. Her hair is the colour of shore sand, curled by the warmth of the lights and the stocking cap.

As we visited, seventeen-month-old Tabatha circled the room, babbling a lovely flow of words, some of them understandable, touching things, bending down, standing up, patting Dinah Jane when she was out and pointing to her when she wasn't. "Ah baby ah!"

She didn't seem interested in me at all. Benjamin kept his distance, too.

"Do you want to cuddle with Nana?" Amanda asked him.

He looked me over from his vantage point in Kendall's arms.

"No," he answered, decisively.

Awhile later he changed his mind.

"Let's walk, Nana," he said, hopping down from Kendall's lap, grabbing my hand and leading me from the room.

I took him where we had gone before, to the hospital basement. Down the long cream halls under a network of pipes (hot water in there, Nana) past the cafeteria (let's go in there, Nana) and all the way to the same little garden (I can play in dirt, Nana?) where we visited five or so months ago when Rick was a patient there.

And in that solarium we hopped on the cement circles, dug a hole in the stones, tried to build a tiny inuksuk, smelled the Norfolk pine tree, looked for birds (found none), and talked about everything and nothing. It only took fifteen minutes or so, but when we surfaced, he wanted me to carry him back down the hall to Mama's room.

I'm back at the parsonage now. Moses greeted me tonight as though he knew I was coming. He has always had a second sense, that cat.

Sunday, February 10

After four days back in Yorkton, preparing the house for Rick's return home and getting acquainted with Dinah Jane, I'm back in my little cement hostel room. Little did I know when we arrived five months ago that this room would become my home for so long. I will miss it, I'm afraid.

Rick expected me. He didn't expect that the entire Buhler clan would accompany me. But how could they not come? Today is his fifty-fifth birthday. We gave him a gift, wrapped in the silken skin of an infant: Dinah Jane.

Benjamin was the first to reach Rick's room. I rounded the corner behind him, eager to hear his birthday greetings to his grandfather. Amanda had been priming him.

"Benjamin, what will you say to Gampa?"

"Happy Day Day, Gampa," he responded, every time.

I watched as he ran up to the Rick's bed, looked up at him, opened his mouth, and said, "Gampa, you got stuck in the bathtub!"

Four days earlier, I had showed Benjamin those pictures of Rick's failed attempt to conquer the tub.

So many have waited for news of Dinah's birth and have been eager to see her. Staff, patients, family.

SUNNY SIDE UP
February 20

Maggie's Assignment Pays Off

The flock of women standing nearby couldn't believe their eyes. The door to elevator four opened and a patient in a wheelchair rolled out: a large gray-bearded man, cradling a doll. The

Preacher. He drifted past their startled silence like a weathered rowboat avoiding a cluster of yachts.

He told me about it after his worst pangs of embarrassment diminished, after I found him parked in the concourse, still holding the doll.

"Hey, this is a rehab hospital, not a mental institution," I said, not kindly, as startled as those women must have been. "What's with the doll?"

"This is my latest Occupational Therapy assignment," he sniffed, offended.

Errin, his physical therapist, has been cooperating with God in the business of restoring function to the Preacher's legs after his attack of West Nile disease six months ago. Maggie, his occupational therapist, has been doing the same with his half-paralyzed left arm. She gives him real-life tasks sometimes, to prepare him for the years ahead outside these healing halls.

So when she learned that our daughter and son-in-law were expecting our third grandchild soon, Maggie delivered unto the Preacher a baby. A doll — very lifelike, very heavy.

"Practice with this," she said.

A fellow patient christened the doll "Junior," and for days, until his arm became accustomed to its weight (and his ego to the pointed stares and raised eyebrows), the Preacher obediently toted it around. Everywhere.

"Has the real baby arrived yet?" people kept asking, but our youngest grandbean decided to wait. After Amanda's second trip to the hospital, her second night in false labour, her second disappointment, she e-mailed me.

"I thought I would have a baby by now, but I'm going home with empty arms."

I ached for her.

A few nights later, just after three a.m., my phone rang. "Labour ... fast ... hospital ... van ..."

The connection wasn't good, but I recognized our son-in-law's voice, understood, and began praying.

Fifty minutes later, the phone jangled again. Kendall, jubilant: "A girl!"

"Praise Father, Son, and Holy Ghost!" I whooped, and well before breakfast rushed over to the ward to tell the Preacher. He scribbled a note: "It's a Girl!" it read. Then he added Dinah's name and weight and pinned it to his chest.

When friends and staff asked, "Any baby yet?" he merely pointed to his chest and grinned.

Less than a week later, Dinah Jane led the entire clan to the rehab centre to wish her grandfather a happy birthday. Around the wards he went, her tiny form nestled in the crook of his arm, just as Maggie had assigned.

The husband of a fellow patient enduring immense difficulties approached the Preacher the next day.

"Seeing that baby was the best thing that's happened to my wife since coming here," he said.

To change the world, add one baby. As God knows very well, babies are very powerful people.

Thursday, February 14
E-mail Update

Family and Friends,

It's been terrible, it's been wonderful. And it's all but over. This Wascana in West Nile chapter, at least.

Today I packed up our two rooms — Rick's on the ward and mine in the hostel. Then I wrote notes of gratitude until my hand cramped, lowered the lift containing my patient husband into the big tub for the last time, purchased the equipment needed to overcome the residue of his disability, hugged a thousand patients and nurses — and one exceptionally caring young doctor — and cried and laughed with most of our split-second friends.

Then I retreated to my hostel room and sat on the edge of the bed a very long time, thinking: Is this when I get to bawl? And whom do I call if I can't stop?

Tomorrow night my husband and I will crawl under the same set of sheets for the first time in six months. Tomorrow night we'll be home.

"Are you scared?" Craig pointed to the words on his word board last night as I prepared my dinner in the hostel kitchen.

"I'd be lying if I said no," I told him. He looked at me, his sea-blue eyes reflecting a pain all his own. A chapter in his life is over, too, and well he knows it. His champions are leaving the arena, and we can't take him along.

His champions are apprehensive.

On Wednesday, Rick's team, in consultation with Rick and me, decided that, yes, patient Richard Gibson is ready for a conditional discharge. We'll return to Yorkton on Friday evening, February 15, one hundred and seventy-seven days since the pirates first attacked. One hundred and seventy-seven x's on two calendars.

If all goes well on the weekend, we will stay in the house we called home before we began accidentally referring to our little rooms at the rehab centre that way.

Rick and I have found, in these healing halls, people whose circumstances have forced them, and all those making the journey with them, to look at life from a radically different perspective. An upside down perspective that has revealed something startling:

The life to which I've often referred to in these letters as our real life is merely a figment of our imagination. A reflection on the surface of calm water: lovely and unbroken until the wind blows, or a passerby throws in a careless stone.

In the midst of the kind of brokenness we've seen and experienced, we've caught a glimpse of true reality, and it looks like this: We are, without exception, fragile people. Easily broken, often floundering, desperately needy, and tremendously resilient — but only by the loan of God's gracious strength, whether or not we consciously seek it.

We're not the only ones in transition. As Cliff pointed out a few weeks ago, "Everybody's going their own way now." Among the people I've written about, those who have fought similar pirates at similar times here in these healing halls, the goodbyes began days ago.

Jen's gone over to long-term care already — a temporary situation for her. She'll soon be living in an apartment of her own, with help.

Irwin and Herb have been discharged to live in the hostel and return as outpatients for as long as they need therapy to adjust to their new prostheses.

Don and Glenda Bell have gone home, too. Don's remembering how to operate his tractor these days, much harder with a walker in tow.

It's a little like the last days at summer camp. The farewells to staff. The prayers with and well wishes for fellow patients who can't leave yet. The flurry of exchanged addresses, the photo-ops. (These aren't school pictures, hon, says Rick. Oh yes they are, says me. The school of hard knocks.)

We know in our hearts that soon this closeness will be impossible: finding others near us who truly understand this kind of upheaval, this realization of fragility, this appalling physical uncertainty.

Strength for all your todays, hope for all your tomorrows,
Rick and Kathleen

Friday, February 15

Rick and I have spent our last day in the healing halls of Wascana Rehabilitation Centre.

District superintendent Larry Dahl came through on his way to Yorkton for our church's board meeting tomorrow. Since he came right at afternoon therapy time, we invited him to join us.

Larry quizzed Maggie on Rick's health. What he learned will help him, he says. He's working on a detailed, gradual return-to-ministry plan, tailored to allow Rick to continue to heal.

The six-member board will vote on three scenarios: (1) Discontinue Rick's current status as pastor and begin looking for another. (2) Wait three months to see the status of his health before making a permanent decision regarding his position. (3) Choose to continue with him as pastor of the church, carrying on with an interim pastor until he heals enough to return full-time.

Oh, Lord, hang on to us all.

∽

"I can fit it all," I said to Rick as I packed up his wardroom, "but I don't think there's room for you."

Craig had parked himself in the doorway, watching as I heaped the luggage cart high.

"What d'ya think, Craig?" I asked him. "Shall I leave him here?" He pumped his yes hand hard.

Cliff walked his chair down to Rick's room.

"I wanna shake your hand, Pastor," he said.

He moved his index finger, strained with all his might to lift his tattooed arm off his chair table.

Rick reached out, grabbed it, and shook it.

Then Cliff said, "An' I wanna shake your woman's hand, too."

He pushed his chair forward and I walked over.

"Oh no you don't," I said. "I'm not shaking your hand. I'm going for a hug."

I encircled him in a tight grip, and had barely released him when he suddenly began pedalling.

"Gotta go t'da can."

We didn't see him again.

Craig could barely say goodbye to Rick. In the last months, the two men have shared long hours of conversation and quiet companionship. Rick has promised to return — he will keep that promise.

Craig pumped his right arm and he reached out (as he already had, several times) to me for a hug.

"Craig, you're the best thing God had waiting for us here at Wascana," I told him.

Up came that spastic muscled arm. And down came that spastic muscled arm. We watched his thumb slide across the letter board one last time.

"You helped me."

SUNNY SIDE UP
February 27, 2008

Preparing for Unexpected Opportunity

I'm writing this column in my own wee office. The one with the Manitoba maple outside the window. The office in the parsonage that has sheltered the Preacher and me for almost seventeen years, watched our children reach adulthood, and welcomed guests from around the world.

We returned here six months after the pirates of West Nile disease attacked the Preacher, eventually sending us into exile to Wascana Rehabilitation Centre. Tied the little boat of our lives at the dock from which we launched. Battle weary, but victorious. God — friend, healer, provider — came along. That's his habit.

We'll reconnect with friends left behind. Tell the stories of what God did in our last half-year. Joyfully enter the next chapter of this miraculous healing journey, which will include ongoing therapy.

But be patient, please. Our hearts are all a-shuffle.

We left friends behind at Wascana, too. The farewell-ing took several days, and it flattened us, like an ice-cream carton after the last spoonful of sweetness has been scraped away. Silence encircled us as our car gulped back the 200 kilometers between the rehab centre and home.

We arrived after dark, slipped silently into the parsonage, unnoticed but for Moses, our great white cat. He met us at the door, stuck his tail in the air, and huffed off.

Above the door leading to the kitchen, our daughter had hung a Welcome Home poster. I didn't notice it until after the final of four hundred and thirty-three trips from car to house, hauling in the detritus of our long absence.

Ah, home. Since our return we've enjoyed our entire family, played with the grandbeans, and made peace with our offended cat — he thought we had died, willed the place to him, and arranged for his servants. We've also been ushered to the threshold of unexpected opportunity.

Within hours of our homecoming, our church board held a lengthy meeting to determine the future direction of the church. After considering their options, they made the difficult decision to carry on without the Preacher. We understood this possibility all along.

Before our district superintendent arrived at the parsonage to deliver their decision, God had cloaked us both with a supernatural sense of inner calm. Just as he did during the last six months, he reassured us that our future rests firmly in his sovereign hands.

The Preacher hasn't been "let go" by anyone. He's been released by God to follow and serve in a new and different way, and the miracle will continue. God, as is also his habit, will work all these things out for his and our best.

During the next three months, we'll move into a different house in our beloved community. A God-provided house. Already it welcomes us home.

There we'll both heal. There we'll welcome family, friends, and former congregation members. There I'll finish the book I've begun. And from there our little boat will launch into a new current of opportunity.

We can't wait to see what God has planned.

Epilogue

May 2008

For years, Rick helped plan the community-wide Good Friday service sponsored by the evangelical ministerial. When the ministerial learned that their absentee president would return in time for Easter, they invited him to speak.

He agreed, and we began praying that the Holy Spirit would inspire him, that the pirates wouldn't interfere, and that God would get the glory for anything that emerged from the day.

When we walked into the theatre, a surprise greeted us. Mom Gibson had flown in from two provinces east to rejoice with us in what God has done in Rick's life and body. For three days, the Beans and their parents had been hiding her in their house. My sister and brother-in-law, Beverly and Bruce Bauman, with their son, Jeremy, and his wife, Sylvia, had already travelled in from two provinces west to help us move.

Only Anthony was missing, though he would have loved to have joined us.

Our family took up almost an entire row in that 750-seat theatre, most of them occupied. My heart soared and bowed simultaneously as I realized how God had touched and healed us — body and soul — through many of these people, most of them strangers.

After the last cadence of the last worship song faded, the congregation sat and the lights lowered. Pools of light illuminated three rough crosses onstage, and quiet filled our spirits. I could hear Rick's walker as he began making his way onstage from behind the curtains, stage left.

As he emerged from the blackness into the light, tracing a slow path toward the tall stool placed near the middle cross, I sensed a shift in the congregation. They began whispering. Rustling.

When the clapping began, he didn't seem to know what to do. Then cheers joined the claps. When those became whistles I looked around in time to see the crowd, almost as one, beginning to rise.

They clapped for what seemed forever. Rick sat on the stool, looking bewildered, embarrassed. I could tell.

But we'd already worked that through. "Not to us, O LORD, not to us but to your name be the glory," we had read in the Psalms earlier.

I rose, too, clapping not only for my husband's courageous spirit and his willingness to be used this way — and so soon — but for the great God who had provided strength and hope for each day and was allowing us to pass it on to others.

We sat again, and listened. Rick told stories that day, stories of people like himself who needed hope — and how God provided it.

We didn't know it then, but a recording of his words by The Rock, a local radio station, would travel far beyond the brick walls of that theatre, farther than we could ever have imagined when we asked God to use our experience for his glory. Not farther, though, than he knew all along.

Come back with me to Hanna, Alberta, in June 2005, almost three years prior.

It didn't look like our kind of church. It had no denominational label, just a simple sign, announcing, rather generically, New Life Community Fellowship. And among the people clustered on the stairs leading into the building, I noticed someone smoking. Besides, it was pink. Strange colour for a church.

But it seemed the only church open in that small town that Sunday, and churchgoing was a bit of a habit for our family, including the baby among us.

Rick and I, Amanda and Kendall, and Benjamin, barely three months old, had driven through the night, making our way to the West Coast to visit family. We needed the break. So even though we weren't dressed in church clothes, we stopped to worship — or so we hoped.

We parked the van, and walked up the stairs into that little pink church. But not before I noticed the car parked directly in front. Its bumper sticker read, "Get in, sit down, hold on, and shut up!"

I nudged Kendall. "Guess we better do what it says, huh?"

The congregation had just taken a short coffee break before the sermon, a friendly woman explained. The members welcomed us warmly, showed us a row of seats, and the service resumed. They had finished the music part, but judging by the drums, instruments, and sound equipment up front, we'd missed some lively singing. Likely some hand raising and clapping, too. I couldn't help thinking about the congregation we'd left behind, where even lifting a hand during worship raised eyebrows.

I don't remember much about the sermon. But after the closing prayer, a young man walked over to our pew, introduced himself as the associate pastor, and quietly asked if he could talk to Rick. The Holy Spirit had impressed things on his heart during the sermon, he said, and he felt compelled to share them.

We haven't practiced our faith that way, over our years as Christ-followers. Our practice has always been seeking God's guidance through his Word, through circumstances, in prayer, and through the counsel of godly friends.

This man knew nothing about any of us; we had no reason to trust whatever he was about to say. But there was something about his eyes. They looked into ours with such kindness and compelling strength.

Rick looked back, then nodded.

In friendly and conversational tones, that young pastor began speaking, his words clear and simple. When he finished talking to Rick,

he turned to me. He spoke several times about our family's "ministry."
We realized later that no one had introduced us. He had no reason to know our profession.

After we left that church, I took a notepad from my purse and wrote down as many of his words as I could recall. Later, I transcribed them into my diary, promptly forgot them, then lost track of the notepad.

Just a few nights before the Good Friday service, as I worked in my office, sorting and packing things for the move to our new home, I suddenly found myself staring at something in my hand: the tiny slip of paper on which almost three years earlier I had written down the young pastor's words. I didn't recall finding it or even picking it up. I began reading, and rushing into my heart came that young man's face and his words to Rick:

"You are a faithful man, a man under authority. God is preparing to release you to wider ministry ..."

The exact phrase we'd used when we told people of our church board's decision to ask for Rick's resignation.

What began that Good Friday morning hasn't stopped since. God has given both Rick and me opportunities abundant to share our journey of faith with thousands.

January 2009

I overheard Rick say to people in the closing days of our time at the rehab centre, "You know, if I leave here walking, I'll be ecstatic. If I have to go home using a walker, I'll be just as happy. And if I still need a wheelchair, I'll be thrilled to have that wheelchair!"

When we returned home, six months after Rick's mosquito bite, he was walking with a walker, and his left arm was still paralyzed from the shoulder to the elbow.

Where is Rick in his recovery today? We're told that his body may never return to his pre-pirate state of health. He's still taking therapy at this writing, still using a walker — and still telling his story, with joy and gratitude. His speaking ministry has expanded to include varied opportunities in several provinces and over local radio. I often join him.

Our "triumph over a deadly disease" lies, in part, in knowing that our Heavenly Father delights in us wherever and whoever we are, no matter our state. I love the message in Psalm 147:10,11, one that is especially appropriate for people struggling with disability: "His pleasure is not in the strength of the horse, nor his delight in the legs of a man; the LORD delights in those who fear him, who put their hope in his unfailing love."

I began this book with a story of three broken-winged birds. During the long months of Rick's illness and therapy, the image of all three of those birds returned to me repeatedly.

The way they had resigned themselves to their affliction, even though it seemed doubtful they would ever fly again.

The way those two guardian geese flanked the third, showing genuine concern for their injured companion.

The way the waxwing, with sweet trust and innocence, allowed my big hand into the cage to hang its daily apple. The way it stilled when I cradled its body in my hand to unsnarl the matted feathers in its jaunty crest. The way its melodic trills kept emerging, even from behind bars.

In spite of the pirates, we began living the lessons of the three birds. Even in the midst of brokenness, of loss and separation from the dear old familiar things we once clung to, we learned we could trust God to provide exactly what we needed, when we needed it: Therapists and medical staff with healing hands. Friends and family who prayed with us and for us. Complete strangers who encouraged us even in the midst of their own battles and busy lives. Finances more than sufficient to meet our needs.

Most important of all, as our little boat negotiated the Nile, we had opportunities to experience the reality of God in a way we never had before. That reality helped us find our own song even in a strange and painful place.

I don't believe in coincidences. I do believe in God-incidents — like this one:

At one of our speaking engagements, following a divine nudge, I made the impromptu decision to tell, for the first time publicly, the story of the three broken-winged birds.

In the audience that day sat the friends who own Tranquil Acres, the lakeside cottage where we had seen the second disabled bird. Norm Manweiler and his wife, Carmen, live across the yard from the cottage, but they had been in the next province visiting family at the time.

Following our presentation, Norm approached me, a smile stretching across his face.

"You know that goose you were talking about?" he said. "He flew away with the rest of his flock in mid-November."

∽

This last lesson, added serendipitously, came as God's gentle reminder never to rule out the possibility of healing and recovery.

Everyone endures periods of loss. Perhaps you've been fighting your own pirates — or monsters, or madmen, or beasts — as you've read this book. (And if you're not, one day you will. Prepare well.)

In the midst of your battles, remember to grab on to faith. Our joint times of prayer and the bracing words we read in scripture provided strength in the midst of our weakness. Faith enabled us to find God in the shadows, stars in the dark, laughter and music in times of mourning, and beauty in the midst of brokenness.

It can do the same for you.

God is greater than the pirates. Life may never replace the treasure the villains steal, but faith enables a different perspective: the understanding that, as scripture repeatedly demonstrates, difficult experiences can produce treasure of a different sort.

Always look for hope. It will rise from unexpected places to lift you. Inhabit it. Listen to its voice. Whatever the outcome of your brokenness, you will laugh again. You will find new beginnings at the blunt end of your experiences — even new treasure to invest in the lives of others. Your soul, reassembled, will reflect loveliness. And you may even fly again.

About West Nile Disease and West Nile Neurological Disease

Some of my readers, particularly those curious about West Nile disease, may have picked up this book hoping for more information. How I wish I could tell you about a cure, a vaccine, even certain protection. None of these exist. I can, however, point you to more information. In what follows, I'll share some of what Rick and I have learned about our pirates along our journey down West Nile. Please keep in mind that we are not medical experts, and that the information here, though thoroughly checked, should not be considered authoritative.

In 2007, the year of Rick's infection, the province of Saskatchewan had the dubious distinction of leading the provinces in Canada in the number of confirmed West Nile disease cases: 1,456. (Please see Saskatchewan link below if you wish to verify this number.)

Of those 1,456 cases, 113 people in the province, like Rick, were diagnosed with the most serious type of West Nile disease, West Nile neurological disease (WNND, also sometimes referred to as West Nile neuroinvasive syndrome). Unlike the more common, milder, flu-like form of the disease, WNND creates neurological complications, such as encephalitis, meningitis, and poliomyelitis (see definitions, below).

It is not understood why the same virus affects some people neurologically and most less severely. Even among those with WNND, symptoms vary. Rick had one of the worst cases in the province that summer, but others were affected even more severely. A few died, and at least one, our friend Isabel Barnsley, remains at Wascana, still recovering at the time of this writing, January 2009.

West Nile disease is not confined to Canada. The first confirmed cases in North America occurred in New York in 1999. Dozens were affected, and the virus caused several deaths, horrifying the medical community and state. The virus was found to have migrated (likely hitching a ride on birds) from Africa.

The West Nile virus (WNV) itself is an arbovirus, one of the viruses passed from host insects, such as mosquitoes and ticks, to the birds, horses, and humans they bite. Prior to arriving in North America from Africa, the virus was also present in the Middle East and West and Central Asia. Since the 1960s, Europe has recorded outbreaks and isolated cases in humans and horses.

Since arriving in North America, the virus — carried (most commonly) by the late-summer culex tarsalis mosquito — has diminished the songbird population and killed numerous horses. But its greatest cost has been to thousands of people across the continent. If you have been paying this price, our hearts and prayers go out to you as you seek answers and strength to carry on.

While the vast majority of people who contract the virus will have only mild symptoms, the neurological form of the disease can devastate its hosts. For those people and families affected, WNND remains a perplexing, heartbreaking condition, sorely lacking in publicity and understanding.

Because of its short North American history, no long-term case studies of those affected have been completed. Indicators suggest that even in non-neurological cases of West Nile disease, many people experience ongoing health complications for years, including tiredness, weakness, and fatigue.

Symptoms of positive West Nile virus infection frequently appear flu-like, and, as in Rick's case, are often wrongly diagnosed because of their similarity to lesser infections. They may include violent headaches, nausea, rash, and weakness. Positive West Nile diagnoses can be determined only by blood tests.

The virus may also cause a coma and/or extreme pain, breathing difficulties, twitches, weakness, fatigue, and diminished sight and hearing. In its most extreme forms, it can generate encephalitis, poliomyelitis, and acute flaccid paralysis, among other conditions (see below). It may even cause death.

Researchers have developed an equine (horse) vaccination, but at the time of this printing, no human vaccination is available to the public. Prevention remains the best safeguard against infection: avoiding areas of high mosquito populations, using repellents, netting, mosquito traps, and removing any standing water on one's property. Old tires, unused shallow pools, even upturned bottle caps become excellent breeding grounds.

As the medical community gains more experience with West Nile disease, more information is emerging. Several long-term studies have begun since Rick's infection. Medical journals, libraries, and websites are all accessible to those who ask. If you or a member of your family is struggling with West Nile disease, either neurological or non-neurological, we encourage you to look the pirates in the eye! It's the best way to fight them.

Conditions that may accompany WNND

Encephalitis: inflammation of the brain.

Meningitis: inflammation of the lining of the brain and spinal cord.

Meningoencephalitis: inflammation of the brain and its surrounding membrane.

Acute flaccid paralysis: a sudden onset of weakness in the limbs and/or breathing muscles due to the development of West Nile poliomyelitis. (While many persons with West Nile disease experience fatigue and feel weak all over, this is not the same as acute flaccid paralysis.)

Poliomyelitis: an inflammation of the spinal cord that causes a syndrome similar to that caused by the poliovirus, often involving paralysis.

Resources for further research
West Nile Story by Dickson Despommier
Dr. Despommier is an infectious disease ecologist with a strong interest in West Nile virus epidemics in the United States. *West Nile Story* explains the history and nature of the virus, and tracks its outbreaks. Available from Amazon.com.

Following our return from Wascana, Rick and I organized a West Nile Awareness evening for our own community. As part of the program, we invited six families affected by the disease (neurological or non-neurological) to sit on a survivors panel and tell their stories. Among others, the panel included Rick and me, Don and Glenda Bell, and Catherine Barnsley (the daughter of Isabel Barnsley, mentioned above). As far as we know, the gathering was the first of its kind in the world. The evening was informal, but the stories, told in quiet tones in response to Chaplain Jim's questions, powerfully portrayed the devastation West Nile can have on people's lives.

Access Communications of Yorkton videotaped the program that evening. They have graciously allowed me to state that the DVD is available for those who may wish a copy, for a small cost of production, shipping and handling. If you are involved in the medical field, this video could prove an especially invaluable resource. Please check my website for more information on how to obtain it.

Online resources:
CANADA
   Public Health Agency of Canada:
   WNV Monitor: www.phac-aspc.gc.ca/wnv-vwn/index-eng.php
   WNV Surveillance Information: www.cnphi-wnv.ca/healthnet/
      Welcome.do

Government of Saskatchewan West Nile Virus Surveillance Results:
www.health.gov.sk.ca/wnv-surveillance-results

USA

Centers for Disease Control:
WNV Monitor: www.cdc.gov/ncidod/dvbid/westnile/index.htm
WNV Surveillance information: www.cdc.gov/ncidod/dvbid/westnile/surv&controlCaseCount08_detailed.htm

UK

Health Protection Agency:
www.hpa.org.uk. Search for publications related to West Nile virus in the UK and WNV surveillance information.

Resources for those suffering from WNND and their families

The West Nile Survivors Foundation: (www.westnilesurvivor.com) includes stories, blogs (westnilesurvivorstories.blogspot.com/), and information.

ABOUT
KATHLEEN
GIBSON
www.kathleengibson.ca

Kathleen and Rick make their home in Saskatchewan, Canada, where there are only two seasons: winter and mosquitoes. Kathleen writes and speaks with transparency and humour, drawing richly from her lifelong Christian faith and over three decades of parsonage living, shared with her pastor husband, two children, and numerous pets. Her words have found homes in media outlets worldwide, including Reader's Digest Global, CBC Radio, and *Homemaker's* magazine. For almost a decade, Kathleen has written "Sunny Side Up," a weekly faith and life column published in *Yorkton This Week* and online. She has taught numerous writing and journaling workshops, and is currently editor of *Prairies North*, Saskatchewan's magazine for good prairie living (www.prairies north.com). Access "Sunny Side Up" and more at www.kathleengibson.ca. Contact Rick or Kathleen at kathleen@kathleengibson.ca

Printed in the United States
137663LV00001B/6/P